Alexander W. Wayman

Cyclopaedia of African Methodism

Alexander W. Wayman

Cyclopaedia of African Methodism

ISBN/EAN: 9783744757645

Printed in Europe, USA, Canada, Australia, Japan

Cover: Foto ©ninafisch / pixelio.de

More available books at **www.hansebooks.com**

CYCLOPÆDIA

OF

AFRICAN METHODISM

BY

ALEXANDER W. WAYMAN,

ONE OF THE BISHOPS OF THE AFRICAN METHODIST EPISCOPAL CHURCH.

BALTIMORE:
Methodist Episcopal Book Depository,
D. H. CARROLL, Agent,
168 W. Baltimore Street.
1882.

Entered according to Act of Congress, in the year 1882, by
A. W. WAYMAN,
In the Office of the Librarian of Congress, at Washington, D. C.

PREFACE.

THE AFRICAN METHODIST EPISCOPAL CHURCH is a public institution among the colored people of America that wields a greater influence than any other institution under their control. It has grown from time to time until it has made a history that is replete with solid facts. Church societies have been organized, church edifices have been built, educational plans have been formed, and many other edifying projects, under the auspices of this great Ecclesiastical body, among the colored people of America have been brought into existence and sustained for the benefit of all mankind. The organization has steadily grown from 1816 up to the present time 1882, and now extends North, South, East and West, and has a national reputation. But this is not all: advancing still under the supervision of the Almighty, it is fast gaining a cosmopolitan reputation and is being respected in common with all other great religious bodies. Its history, therefore, succinct or *in extenso*, embraces such a number of interesting facts as are of importance to the reading world, and should be given to it. And so this volume, termed "THE CYCLOPÆDIA OF AFRICAN METHODISM," is designed to convey its readers to places where meeting houses have been built and to introduce them to clerical and lay members who have worked conspicuously in forwarding the great interests of the connection.

Within the range of this work it will be ascertained that the leading character in the establishment of the organization was the distinguished Richard Allen, who was set apart as the first Bishop. His labors and fidelity are clearly set forth, and a brief account is given of the twelve other bishops who have succeeded him. This is an interesting part of the work within itself; for it is the presentation of men who have been recognized as representatives amid all the circumstances of the Church.

In connection with their history, true narratives are given of those who have labored as elders, deacons and licentiates. Something will be learned of those who were and those who are eccentric, of those who have performed their duties with great earnestness, persistency and success, even to the end of their existence; of those who now "bear the burden in the heat of the day," and are struggling for the mastery over the adversary of men's souls. Their intellect, learning and religion, their efficiency as pastors, their power as preachers, and their skillfulness as leaders in the Church of God are considered here according to their merit. The outlines of those who figured in the history of the Church, in its incipiency, and of those who are doing so in the present day, as African Methodist Episcopal ministers of Christ's Gospel, are given here to be read, understood and appreciated by those who are seeking information.

And then, too, knowledge is given here of individuals, local preachers, class-leaders, stewards, trustees, choir-leaders, Sabbath School superintendents and sextons, which the world cannot gain from any source except the pages of this volume. Here the good and noble deeds of faithful men and women of this Church are disinterred from the sepulchre which, for generations, has kept them concealed from our observation. They are brought forth, the deeds of the dead and those of the living, that they may illustrate the sincerity of those who have finished their course, and of those who are yet toiling on as African Methodists in the vineyard of our Lord. Persons, times and places in this peculiar circle of knowledge are all given in connection with their history of African Methodism in the United

States of America, that it may be seen how great has grown the little scion from the mighty trunk of the present day.

Then reader, scan the pages well, walk with those who live, view the course of those who are no more, look at the monuments built to the glory of God's name and own that no branch of His Church is formed in vain.

J.

BALTIMORE, MD., June 6th, 1882.

INTRODUCTION.

THE AUTHOR, in presenting this work to the public, believes that he is doing that which will be of lasting interest to the Church he represents. Animated by a preconception of the attending good results, he has employed the spare moments between the periods for the regular discharge of his official duties to gather in the material which makes up the contents of his book.

In doing this he has been compelled to labor with great assiduity to be successful in the undertaking. A great number of facts had to be gathered in from all parts of the land, and, at the same time, such labors had to be performed as those which belong to the episcopacy of the African Methodist Episcopal Church. And so it is seen at once that this task has been something more than "child's play." It is believed, though, that the interest taken by the reading classes in the general character of the work will amply repay him for his many days of toil and anxiety to bring it into existence. Consoled by this anticipation, he submits it to all readers, with the hope that every page perused will furnish a stock of such information as will be useful, pleasing and edifying. He believes that if this end should be attained, the work will have been truly done to the glory of God.

J.

CYCLOPÆDIA

OF

AFRICAN METHODISM.

BISHOPS OF THE A. M. E. CHURCH.

ALLEN, RICHARD — the first Bishop of the A. M. E. Church, was born a slave in Delaware, and raised in Pennsylvania; was licensed to preach in the M. E. Church; was ordained first by Bishop Asbury of the M. E. Church in 1799, and was therefore the first colored man ordained by Mr. Asbury. He was elected Bishop in 1816, and died in Philadelphia, Pa., on the 26th of March, 1831. The first Conference he attended was in Baltimore, Maryland, after he was elected Bishop. It had been announced in the papers that the Bishop of the A. M. E. Church would preach on Sunday morning. When the time came a great congregation turned out. It is said by those who were present that he fell a little below the expectation of the many hearers. At the close of the sermon Rev. Daniel Coker rose up and said, " While Bishop Allen was not such a great preacher, he was a very useful man, and calculated to do a great deal of good." After the close of the sermon at night, Bishop Allen rose up and took another text—Rev. xx, 12: "And I saw the dead small and great stand before God,"—and preached with power. When he closed he descended from the pulpit and dropped upon his knees in the altar. It was said by an eye-witness that the scepter departed from Rev. Daniel Coker that night.

BROWN, MORRIS—the second Bishop of the A. M. E. Church, was born in Charleston, South Carolina. Soon after his conversion he entered the M. E. Church and was licensed to preach. He remained there until the organization of the A. M. E. Church, in Philadelphia, Pa. He was delegated by the colored members of the M. E. Church to visit Philadelphia to see Bishop Allen, and if approved of by the Conference, he was to be ordained and returned to Charleston to organize an A. M. E. Church. Upon his arrival in Philadelphia he was gladly received by Bishop Allen, and the Conference elected and ordained him Deacon and Elder. When he returned to Charleston, South Carolina, he organized the A. M. E. Church and in a short time had fifteen hundred members. About this time an insurrection broke out in South Carolina, headed by a man by the name of Denmark Vessey. The ministers of Morris Brown's Church were suspected of being *particeps criminis*. The white friends of Morris Brown advised him to leave Charleston, South Carolina. He was therefore placed on board of a ship and sent to Philadelphia, Pa., and engaged in the business of boot and shoe making. In 1828 he was elected and ordained Bishop. He used to cross over the Alleghany Mountains on horse-back to attend the Western Conferences. While attending the Annual Conference in Canada, in 1844, he was paralyzed and was brought home by his old friend and brother, Rev. N. C. W. Carmon. He died in May 1850.

WATERS, EDWARD — third Bishop of the A. M. E. Church, was born a slave at West River, Maryland. He came to Baltimore City when a young man, and joined the A. M. E. Church. He was subsequently ordained Deacon and Elder. He was selected by Bishop Morris Brown as his assistant. At the General Conference which met in Philadelphia, 1836, he was elected Bishop. In the spring of 1847 he was once on his way to an appointment a few miles from Baltimore City, and some reckless young man drove his carriage against him and knocked him to the ground and injured him to such an extent that he never recovered. He died in great peace at his daughter's, Mrs. Margaret Steward.

QUINN, WM. PAUL — the fourth Bishop of the A. M. E. Church, was supposed to have been born in 1788. There are contradictory statements as to the place of his birth. He entered the A. M. E. Church when a young man, after spending several years in New York and Pennsylvania. In 1832 he went over the Alleghany Mountains, and organized churches in Indiana, Illinois, Michigan, Kentucky, Missouri and Iowa. In 1844 he was elected Bishop. Afterward he traveled very extensively East, West, North and South. At the General Conference held at Nashville, May 1872, he was relieved from active work. He afterward visited several conferences. February 1873 he died at his residence in Richmond, Indiana.

NAZREY, WILLIS—the fifth Bishop of the A. M. E. Church, was born in Virginia, where he spent his youth. When he reached manhood he took a notion to follow the sea, which he did for several years. He was converted in New York, and joined old Bethel Church in that city. He was admitted into the New York Conference, 1840, and transferred to the Baltimore Conference and appointed to the Lewistown Circuit in Pennsylvania. He remained in the Baltimore Conference until 1842, when he was transferred to the Philadelphia Conference and remained pastor of some of the most important charges. In 1852 he was elected Bishop. Soon afterward he took up his residence in Canada. When the British M. E. Church of Canada was organized, he was elected their Bishop. He continued to travel extensively until the autumn of 1875, when he finished his course in Nova Scotia, and was brought home to Chatham and buried from the church in that city.

PAYNE, DANIEL ALEXANDER—the sixth Bishop of the A. M. E. Church, was born in Charleston, South Carolina, February 1811. He learned the carpenter's trade, but he felt that the school house was his place, and he established a high school for colored children, and it flourished for some years. The attention of the city authorities were called to what he (Payne) was doing—educating the colored people. He then left his native city for New York, and on reaching there called upon several distinguished ministers, to whom he bore letters of recommendation from other ministers of Charleston, S. C. Among them was a minister of the Lutheran Church, who said to him that the ministers of his Church had been considering the propriety of educating some colored man to preach the Gospel among the colored people in this country, and requested him to go to Gettysburg, Pa., and take a regular course. He accepted the offer and went. When he got through there he was ordained and went to Philadelphia to enter the A. M. E. Annual Conference. He was persuaded by some friend not to do so then, and so he established a high school in Philadelphia, which he taught for some years. In 1842 he joined Bethel Church, Philadelphia, and in 1843 he was admitted into the Conference, and was transferred to the Baltimore Conference and stationed at Israel Church, Washington, D. C. From Washington he went to Baltimore City, and during his term there the large Bethel Church was built. The General Conference of 1848 appointed him to write the history of the A. M. E. Church. In 1852 he was elected Bishop. The degree of D. D. was conferred on him by Wilberforce University. He subsequently became its President. In 1867 he visited Europe. On his return home he engaged actively in the work. While attending the great Ecumenical Council in London in 1881, he presided one day over its deliberations to the satisfaction of all present.

WAYMAN, ALEXANDER W.— the seventh Bishop of the A. M. E. Church, was born in Caroline County, Maryland, September 1821. He was brought up on the farm of his father, who put him to ploughing when he was a little boy. His father had to saw the handles of the plow off so that he could manage it. With this outfit he went to the field. He was once asked by some one after he had grown to be a man, what made him grow so large. His answer was, "My father put me to ploughing when I was young and made my muscles expand, and therefore I grew large." He was taught his letters by his father, and then he began to spell and read. It was not long before he got the idea in his head that he must write. The sand in the roads and the sides of the old frame houses were his copy books. Soon he was writing letters for his young friends to their young friends. In August 1835 he obtained hope in Christ. In 1837 he joined the M. E. Church. In 1840 he united with the A. M. E. Church. In 1843 he was admitted into the Philadelphia Conference. After filling stations in Philadelphia, Baltimore and Washington, D. C., in 1864 he was elected Bishop.

CAMPBELL, JABEZ P.— the eighth Bishop of the A. M. E. Church, was born in Delaware about 1815. When he was quite small his father gave a gentleman a mortgage upon him and then went away, and when the money was due the mortgage was foreclosed, and an attempt was made to sell him, but he got wind of it and left the State of Delaware for Philadelphia, where his mother resided.

He soon became an active member of the A. M. E. Church. After he was licensed to preach he was appointed by Bishop Morris Brown to supply a vacancy on the Bucks County Circuit, Pennsylvania. From there he was sent a missionary to the New England States. He subsequently filled Albany and New York City stations. He was then transferred to the Philadelphia Conference. In 1856 he was elected Editor of the *Christian Recorder*, which position he resigned, and afterward filled the Trenton, New Jersey, Station and Bethel Church, Philadelphia. In 1863 he was transferred to the Baltimore Conference. In May 1864 he was elected Bishop. He was the first Bishop that visited California and organized that Conference. In 1876 the General Conference sent him as a delegate to the Wesleyan General Conference in England. On his arrival he was received and treated with great Christian civility. The degree of D. D. was conferred upon him by Wilberforce University.

SHORTER, JAMES ALEXANDER — the ninth Bishop of the A. M. E. Church, was born in Washington, D. C., February 1817. He learned his trade as a barber in Philadelphia, being placed by his parents under the charge of Rev. Walter Proctor, who looked after him during his apprenticeship. After he finished his trade he left for the West, and went as far as Galena, Illinois, and while out in those western wilds was converted and joined the Church. He subsequently returned to Philadelphia, and was taken into Bethel Church by Bishop Morris Brown.

After his marriage he returned to Washington, D. C., and was received into Israel Church. He was soon licensed to exhort and preach. In April 1846 he was admitted on trial in the Baltimore Conference. He filled prominent stations in that Conference, such as Israel Church, Washington, D. C., and two in Baltimore. In 1857 he was transferred to the Ohio Conference, where he filled important stations. One year he was the agent for Wilberforce University and succeeded admirably. In 1868 he was elected Bishop and organized all the Conferences in the South-West.

WARD, THOMAS M. D.—the tenth Bishop of the A. M. E. Chnrch, was born in Pennsylvania, 1823. His father and mother crossed over the Maryland line only a few months previous to his birth, and therefore he claims to be a Pennsylvanian. At an early age he was converted and admitted into the A. M. E. Church, and soon after moved to Philadelphia, where he was licensed to preach. Subsequently he was admitted into the New England Conference. After being ordained an Elder he was appointed Missionary to the Pacific coast, where he remained for several years and organized churches along the Coast. In 1868 he was elected Bishop and returned to the Pacific Coast, and remained there for four years. Afterward, he was assigned to Georgia, Alabama, Florida and Mississippi, where he distinguished himself as an orator of the first class. The degree of D. D. was conferred upon him by Wilberforce University.

BROWN, JOHN MIFLIN — the eleventh Bishop of the A. M. E. Church, was born in Delaware, September 1817. He left his native state when but a youth and went to Philadelphia, and learned the barber's trade with the late Frederick A. Hinton. After his conversion he united with the A. M. E. Church, in Philadelphia and was licensed. In 1840 he left Philadelphia and went to Oberlin College, in Ohio, where he spent several years. After leaving college, he was engaged as a teacher in Detroit, Michigan. Subsequently he was admitted into the Ohio Conference and appointed Principal of the "Union Seminary." There was a call for a minister to go to New Orleans, Louisiana. The lot fell on him, and he was sent there by Bishop Quinn, and he had the pleasure like Paul, Silas and Peter, to rest in prison many a night in the Crescent City for preaching the Gospel. In 1858 he was transferred to the Baltimore Conference, in which he filled important stations. In 1864 he was elected by the General Conference Corresponding Secretary of the Missionary Society. In 1868 he was elected Bishop, and he has traveled extensively ever since. The degree of D. D. was conferred on him by the Avery College, Alleghany City, Pa.

TURNER, HENRY McNEAL, D. D. LL. D.—the twelfth Bishop of the A. M. E. Church, was born in South Carolina, February 1833, and lived there until he grew up to manhood. He embraced religion in his youth and joined the M. E. Church South, and was licensed to preach. He made a visit to New Orleans, La. Then and there he made the acquaintance of the late Rev. Dr. W. R. Revels, from whom he received some information respecting the existence of the A. M. E. Church. He was admitted into the Missouri Conference in 1858, and transferred by Bishop Payne to the Baltimore Conference. He began soon to rise in the intellectual scale. He was commissioned the first colored Chaplain in the United States army, and was highly honored in this position. On leaving the army he took up his residence in Georgia and organized the A. M. E. Church all over the State. He was also a member of the Constitutional Convention of Georgia and a State Senator, and Presiding Elder. In 1876 he was elected General Business Manager of the Publication Department and served four years. At the end of this term he was elected Bishop, and in addition to his regular Episcopal District he has been assigned to oversee the work in Africa.

DICKERSON, WM. FISHER, D. D.— the thirteenth Bishop of the A. M. E. Church, was born in Woodberry, New Jersey, 1845. He is the son of Rev. Henry and Sophia Dickerson. Both of them were for many years worthy members of the African M. E. Church. W. F. Dickerson was taught the primary branches of education at the little school in his native town, Woodberry, New Jersey. When quite young he went to New York City and was received into the A. M. E. Church, and for some time led the choir. Then feeling it was his duty to preach the Gospel and also the great necessity of being educationally qualified, he entered Lincoln University, Pennsylvania, and graduated. He then entered the New York Annual Conference, and was transferred to the New England Conference. The General Conference of 1876 appointed him one of the fraternal delegates to the General Conference of the M. E. Church in Baltimore. His address before that body was so masterly that it brought down the whole house. Bishop Payne then appointed him to Sullivan Street Church, New York. In 1880 he was elected Bishop and assigned to South Carolina and Georgia work.

CAIN, RICHARD H.—the fourteenth Bishop of the A. M. E. Church, was born in Virginia. Soon after his conversion he gave evidence of future promise. The Church had confidence in his Christian integrity, and gave him license to preach. He was then admitted into the Illinois Conference and filled some prominent stations, such as St. Paul Chapel, St. Louis. In 1860 he went to Wilberforce University, where he spent some time. From there he was appointed by Bishop Payne to the Bridge Street Church, Brooklyn, New York, where he remained until 1865, when he was transferred to the South Carolina Conference by Bishop Wayman and appointed by Bishop Payne to Emmanuel Church, Charleston, South Carolina. In that city he did a grand work. He was elected to the Constitutional Convention which revised the Constitution of the State. He was next elected to the State Senate. He also represented Charleston District twice in the United States Congress. In 1880 he was elected Bishop and assigned to Louisiana and Texas work, and went to it bravely. The Degree of D. D. was conferred on him by Wilberforce University.

A

ABBEVILLE, South Carolina, an important station in the Columbia Conference, has a membership numbering 374 persons.

ABRAHAM, MAY, an Elder in the Columbia Conference.

ACCOO, WILLIAM, was a local preacher of Bethel Church, Philadelphia. He has labored assiduously in that capacity, and now he is old. His last days will be spent at the Old Folks' Home, erected for that purpose by the late Rev. Stephen Smith.

ACCOO, WILLIAM H., a member of the Philadelphia Conference, is the son of William Accoo. He embraced religion when he was young, and at the present time fills the station at Columbia, Pa.

ADAMS, GEO. WASHINGTON, a worthy layman and class leader, was born in Easton, Maryland, about March 4th, 1807. He has lived in Baltimore for many years, and is considered one of the most pious members of Bethel Church.

ADAMS, JAMES P., a layman was born in Easton, Maryland, March 4, 1816. He went to Baltimore when a young man and joined Bethel Church. He subsequently moved to Port Deposit, Maryland, and assisted Rev. Levin Lee in the organization of the A. M. E. Church. He returned back to Baltimore and died in great peace in January 1872.

ADAMS, P. W., an Elder in the North Mississippi Conference.

ADAMS, REMAS, of Catonsville, Baltimore County, Md., a layman in the A. M. E. Church, a man of wealth and influence.

ADDICUSSON, HENRY, an aged member of the Ohio Conference, who died some years ago.

AFRICAN M. E. CHURCH was organized in 1816, in the City of Philadelphia.

ALABAMA CONFERENCE was organized by Bishop Brown, in 1868, at Mobile, Alabama.

AFRICANUS, EDWARD C., was born in the State of New York, 1821. He received a common school education. He was received into the New York Conference in 1843, and being very studious, he soon acquired a knowledge of Latin and Greek and was considered the most talented minister in the New York Conference. His ministerial career was short. He died in 1850, aged 31. His mortal remains sleep in Flushing, Long Island.

ALLANA, THOMAS, a local minister of the A. M. E. Church, who lived, labored and died in Pennsylvania.

ALBANY, capital of New York. The A. M. E. Church was organized in that city many years since by some of the fathers. The Church is in a flourishing condition and is the only Colored Methodist church in the city.

ALEXANDER, JOSEPH H., a member of the Illinois Conference, joined the A. M. E. Church in Iowa, from which State he was recommended to the Annual Conference, and is now an efficient minister in his conference.

ALEXANDER, P. J., an Elder in the Missouri Conference, was born a slave in Kentucky, which State he left and went to Chicago, Illinois. He then united with the A. M. E. Church, and was admitted into the Illinois Conference and then transferred to the Missouri Conference, where he now labors.

ALEXANDER, WELLINGTON G., a young and promising member of the Baltimore Conference, at present is stationed at Frederick City, Maryland.

ALLEN, SARAH, wife of Bishop Allen, who was a great help to her husband, lived to a good old age and passed away very calmly.

ALLEN, H. D., a member of the Columbia Conference.

ALLENTOWN, N. J. The A. M. E. Church was planted in this town more than forty years ago, and is in good condition, having a strong membership.

ALLEGHANY CITY, PA. In this city there is a strong A. M. E. Church. She has had able ministers as pastors, and is regarded as the leading colored church in the city.

ALTON, Illinois, has two A. M. E. churches, one in lower and the other in upper Alton. This is the town where Lovejoy was killed.

ALTOONA, Pennsylvania, has one A. M. E. church, represented to be in a good condition.

AMERICUS, GA. The A. M. E. Church was organized in this city by Rev. M. H. Turner, and is now one of the most flourishing stations in that part of the State.

AMOS, STEPHEN, a local preacher of New York, known and loved for his piety, died at an advanced age.

ANDERSON, JOHN H., a local preacher, was born a slave in Maryland. On leaving there he went to New Jersey, and for a man that has had no educational advantages was considered a remarkable one. He had a very retentive memory. He lived and died in Bushtown, New Jersey.

ANNAPOLIS, Md., the capital of the State. The A. M. E. Church was organized in this city by Rev. John F. Lane, A. D., 1862, and is now in good condition. The building is the largest one owned by the colored people of the city.

ARMSTRONG, JOHN L., a member of the Philadelphia Conference, died in that city 1852.

ARNETT, BENJAMIN WM., a member of the Ohio Annual Conference and the present Financial Secretary of the Church, was born in Brownsville, Pennsylvania. He attended a good school when he was young. After he grew up to manhood, he went to Washington, D. C., and there taught school and was licensed to preach. Upon entering the Conference he filled some of the most responsible stations, and was twice elected Secretary of the General Conference.

ARTIS, WATSON T., a member of the Ohio Conference, was born in North Carolina, May 6, 1841, and was admitted into the Conference 1876.

ARNOLD, WILLIAM R., was born a slave in Maryland. He was converted when young and joined the Church.

Soon after, he was admitted into the Ohio Conference; afterward transferred to the Baltimore Conference, where he is now filling a very important charge.

ARKANSAS CONFERENCE was organized by Bishop Shorter in 1868. It then embraced the whole State, but since then it has been divided into two.

ASBURY, JOHN WESLEY, a member of the Kentucky Conference, and also the Secretary, was born in Ohio. His father was one of the first members of the A. M. E. Church, and he lived to see four of his sons able ministers, viz: John Wesley, Dudley E., Cornelius and Jesse.

ATCHISON, Kansas, is the capital of the county in which it is situated. The A. M. E. Church was organized soon after the State was admitted into the Union. There is a membership of about one hundred.

ANTHONY, WILLIAM, a layman of Philadelphia, a member of Bethel Church, was a trustee for some years.

ANTHONY, JOHN, a layman of New York, was for many years an officer in the A. M. E. Church, and was for many years in the employment of ex-Senator Fish, of New York.

ATHENS is a very fine town in Franklin County, Ga. The A. M. E. Church has about two hundred members here, a flourishing Sunday school, and valuable church property.

ATLANTA, Ga., the capital of the State. The A. M. E. Church was organized there soon after the war. There are three churches in the city, with large memberships. The General Conference of 1876 was held there, and the delegates were well entertained.

ATWATER, W. A., a member of the Alabama Conference, was born in Atlanta, Ga., December 25, 1852, and was admitted into the Conference 1867, and is now stationed at Mobile, Alabama, doing a grand work.

AUSTIN, Texas, was named after Col. Austin. At the close of the late war the flag of African Methodism was raised there. The membership amounts to one hundred, and a large Sunday school.

B

BAGWELL, RICHARD, a local preacher of Philadelphia, Pa., for many years connected with the Zion Mission Church.

BAKER, T. J., Presiding Elder of the Abbeville District, Columbia Conference, South Carolina — a man of great Christian integrity.

BALTIMORE, Md. The A. M. E. Church was organized in this city about A. D. 1816. There are now nine churches in good condition in Baltimore, viz: Bethel, Ebenezer, Water's Chapel, Trinity, St. John, Mount Zion, Allen Chapel, St. Paul and Union Bethel.

BALTIMORE CONFERENCE, one of the oldest in the connection, was organized in 1817. It embraces all the State of Maryland and the District of Columbia; has three Presiding Elders' Districts with fifty-four stations, circuits and missions; fifty-four active ministers, two superannuated and twelve local preachers, who are attached to the Conference.

BALTIMORE, PRISCILLA, is one of the oldest female members of St. Paul A. M. E. church, in St. Louis, Missouri. It was in her house where Bishop Quinn organized the A. M. E. Church in Illinois. She is known as "Mother Baltimore" in many parts of Illinois and Missouri.

BANNISTER, JOHN, a local preacher of Allen Station, Baltimore, was born and raised in Cecil County, Maryland, and died in Baltimore. He was known as the great ballad singer.

BANTON, C. WILLIAMS, a member of the Philadelphia Conference, was born in Philadelphia and has been a clerk in the Book Department for years.

BARNEY, RICHARD, a member of the Philadelphia Conference, was born a slave in the State of Maryland. From there he went to Philadelphia, and united with Bethel Church. It is said that when he felt it was his duty to work in the vineyard of the Master he could not read, but one night while asleep he dreamed that he could read, and next morning when he got up he took the Testament and commenced reading. He was licensed to exhort October 1840, and admitted into the Philadelphia Conference 1848, and died in January 1880. When he was nearing the verge of Jordan he was asked by one brother what he should tell the brethren. He said, " Tell them I meet death with no fear or doubting."

BARBER, JOHN W., a member of the Ohio Conference, was born in Brownsville, Pa. He studied awhile at

Wilberforce University. He is now actively engaged in the Conference.

BASS, JESSE, a member of the Illinois Conference, was born in Illinois.

BASS, L. W., a late member of the Illinois Conference. He died at a good old age.

BASSETT, SHADRACK, the first missionary of the A. M. E. Church that visited the Eastern Shore of Maryland, was born in Maryland, and was ordained by Bishop Allen. He died in Philadelphia at a good age.

BATON ROUGE, La., has an A. M. E. church with about two hundred and seventy-five members and in good condition.

BATTLE CREEK, Mich., has an A. M. E. church, a good membership and an interesting Sunday School.

BAYARD, STEPHEN P., a superannuated member of the Baltimore Conference, was born in Maryland about 1810. He became a member of the A. M. E. Church in his youth, and soon grew in favor with the Church. He was admitted into the Baltimore Conference April 1855. For the last few years he has sustained a superannuated relation to the Conference. He died July 5, 1881.

BAILEY, R. B., a very prominent Elder in the Georgia Conference, is one of the oldest ministers in the Conference.

BAYLEY, GEORGE W., a member of the New York Conference, was born in Maryland. The first years of his ministry were spent among the Union Methodists. He subsequently united with the New York Conference of the

A. M. E. Church, and is now the very efficient missionary of the State of New York.

BECKETT, JOHN WESLEY, a member of the Philadelphia Conference, was born in Georgetown, D. C., and was educated at Wilberforce University. He has since filled prominent stations in the Conference.

BEARD, WILSON, a very intelligent local preacher of Detroit, Michigan, was in the employ of Senator Z. Chandler at the time of his death.

BELL, GEORGE, one of the first members of the A. M. E. Church in Washington, D. C., died at a good old age, loved and respected by all who knew him.

BELLAIRE, OHIO, is situated on the west side of the Ohio River. The A. M. E. Church has existed in this town for several years, and has a membership of sixty-five.

BELLEFONTAINE, Ohio. The A. M. E. Church has a membership of seventy, and a Sunday School of forty scholars.

BELLVILLE, Ill., a fine town. The A. M. E. Church has a membership of sixty, and a Sunday School in good condition.

BELL, JOHN, a member of the Ohio Conference was formerly a member and minister in the Baptist Church. Some years ago he united with the A. M. E. Church; since that time he has been a successful pastor in his Conference.

BENSON, GEORGE W., a member of the Illinois Conference, was born in the State of New York.

BENSON, GEORGE W., of the Indiana Conference, was

born in North Carolina, came to Indiana a young man and joined the A. M. E. Church, and subsequently was admitted into the Indiana Conference.

BENSON, LLOYD, a member of the Baltimore Conference, was a great worker in the cause; died in peace in Frederick, Md.

BEANS, SCIPIO, a member of the Baltimore Conference, was sent out in 1824 as the first missionary to the people of Hayti. He succeeded in planting the standard of Emmanuel there, and for some time he preached the Gospel. Finally disease overtook him and he fell at his post, and now his remains sleep there, awaiting the resurrection of the just.

BEANS, JOHN H., a member of the New Jersey Conference. He is said to be a nephew of the Rev. Scipio Beans, who died in Hayti, and is a very energetic worker.

BERRY, ISHMAEL, a local preacher of Princeton, New Jersey, was one of the men who aided in the organization of the A. M. E. Church in that part of New Jersey. He died some years ago, leaving a large family behind him.

BERRY, RICHARD, a local preacher of Alexandria, Va., removed to Washington City after the war, and held his membership at St. Paul's Chapel. He attended market one day when some one very abruptly assailed him, which very much excited him for the time being. At night he attended a general class and spoke of the trial he had that day, and sat down and in a few minutes died.

BENTLY, SCOTT D., a member of the Kentucky Conference, was born in that state. He is one of the coming young men. He represented his Conference in the General Conference of 1880.

BERRY, GEORGE W., a layman belonging to Bethel Church, Baltimore, was born in Dorchester County. He has served as trustee and leader for many years, and is highly respected by all who know him.

BERRY, JOHN, a layman, was born in Cecil County, Maryland, and was the main support of the A. M. E. Church in that part of the county. He was an extensive farmer, and no man was more respected than he. His death was peaceful.

BERRY, ALEXANDER, a local deacon of Harford County, Md.

BETHEL was the name of the first African M. E. church built in Philadelphia, and is still a favorite name.

BIAS, JAMES, M. D., a local elder of Philadelphia, was born in Maryland. He studied medicine in Philadelphia, and for several years was a successful practitioner. He was a great advocate of temperance and did much for the improvement of his race. He died in Philadelphia, June 1860.

BISHOP, H. WILLIAM, an elder of the North Carolina Conference, was a man of some note. He was one of the first that cast in his lot with the A. M. E. Church.

BLACKSON, SHADRACK, a local preacher of Chester County, Pa., is a well read man for the opportunities he enjoyed. He has worked hard for the Church.

BLAKE, PHATON, one of the old local preachers of

Bethel Church, Baltimore, Md., was regarded as a Christian gentleman.

BLAKE, HENRY, a highly respectable layman of Philadelphia. He went to California and there died.

BLOOMINGTON, Ill. There is one A. M. E. church, with a membership of one hundred, and a fine church property.

BOGGS, JOHN, one of the early ministers of the A. M. E. Church, was a native of Maryland. He filled several important charges. He died in Philadelphia, May 1848.

BOND, LEVIN, a local preacher of New Jersey, was born somewhere in Maryland. He went to New Jersey when he was a young man, and connected himself with the A. M. E. Church, in which he lived and died.

BORDENTOWN, New Jersey, has an interesting church and congregation. When the Church was organized the class was led for some time by a Christian female.

BOSTON, Mass. The A. M. E. Church was organized in this city by Rev. Noah C. W. Cannon, while he was the missionary to the New England States. The Charles Street A. M. E. Church is one of the most imposing church buildings in that city.

BOYER, GEORGE E., a member of the New Jersey Conference, was born in Delaware, and died in Burlington, New Jersey, May 1880.

BOSTON, ROBERT, a very intelligent local deacon, was born in Lancaster, Pennsylvania.

BOWEN, ANTHONY, a local deacon of Washington,

D. C., was for many years employed in the Patent Office, and was once elected a member of the City Council. He was so highly appreciated by the citizens of that part of the city where he lived that they named one of their public schools " Anthony Bowen School House." He died in 1872.

BOON, MOSES, a local deacon of Frederick, Md., was a man of great common sense and uprightness of character.

BOON, ELISHA, an elder in the North Carolina Conference.

BOWLING GREEN, Kentucky. The largest A. M. E. church in the State is located in this city. It was built by Rev. Bartlett Taylor. It has a membership of three hundred.

BOWSER, JACOB W., an elder in the Baltimore Conference, was born in Baltimore City, and has been a success in every charge he has served.

BOWMAN, JEREMIAH, is a member of the West Tennessee Conference, and a minister that stands high among his brethren.

BRADDICKS, HENRY, a layman of Bethel Church, Baltimore, Md. After he joined the Church he served for many years as recording steward, and also as class leader. He was one of the sweetest singers of his day. The last position he filled in the Church was that of a sexton. The whole Church mourned his loss when he passed away.

BRADFORD, THOMAS, a noble Christian layman of Bethel Church, Baltimore, Md., has served for many years as a trustee and leader. He is always at his post. He raised a large family of children and has lived to see them all members of the Church.

BRADWELL, CHARLES L., a presiding elder in the Georgia Annual Conference, was born a slave, learned the trade of blacksmith, and entered the Church in his youth, and was licensed to preach in the M. E. Church South. He was the first preacher that joined the A. M. E. Church in Savannah, Ga.

BRADWELL, WILLIAM, of the Alabama Conference, was born in Darien, Ga., and was admitted into the first Conference held at Savannah, Ga., by Bishop Payne. He was elected to the State Senate of Florida. Since then he has been engaged in the active work of the ministry.

BRAXTON, G. H., a member of the Kansas Conference, is a man that is highly respected wherever he is known.

BRIDGES, RICHARD, a Kentuckian by birth, entered the Indiana Conference when a young man, and after filling several important charges died in the City of Indianapolis, Ind., 1873.

BRIGHT, WILLIAM H., a layman in Baltimore and a steward in the St. John's Church Chapel.

BRIDGEPORT, Conn., a small city. The A. M. E. church there is not a very large building and the membership is rather small.

BRISCO, ELIZABETH, an estimable Christian, is a member of Bethel Church, Baltimore, Md.

BRISTOL, Pa., has a beautiful little A. M. E. church

situated in a pleasant location, with a membership of one hundred.

BROCK, JOHN C., a member of the Philadelphia Conference, was born in Carlisle, Pa., April 12, 1843, was admitted into the Conference May 1876, and was ordained an elder in June 1881. He is a man of fair education.

BROOKINS, J. E., was born in Ga., and died May 8, 1881.

BROOKINS, B. R., a member of the East Florida Conference, was born in Georgia, December 12, 1853.

BROOKLYN, N. Y. The A. M. E. Church has had an existence in this city since 1818. At present there are two flourishing churches and congregations, one situated on Bridge Street and the other on Fleet Street.

BROOKS, BAZELL L., an elder in the Texas Conference, was born in Washington, D. C. He went to Pittsburgh when quite a young man. After being admitted into the Ohio Conference, he filled very important stations. He was then transferred to the Tennessee Conference, where he did a great work. In 1880 he was transferred to the Texas Conference, where he now labors.

BOOTH, GEORGE C., an elder of the Illinois Conference, is one of the finest scholars in the Conference and an able preacher.

BRODIE, GEO. WASHINGTON, an elder in the Baltimore Conference, was born in Kentucky and educated in Cincinnati, Ohio. He filled several prominent positions in the Government and Church.

BROWN, MARCUS, a local deacon of Philadelphia, was a native of Charleston, South Carolina, and was a very exemplary Christian man. He died a peaceful death.

BROWN, WILLIAM H. G., a local elder of Baltimore, was a man of some literary attainment and for years served the Church as its recording steward. He died in the City of Baltimore 1869.

BROWN, HENRY, an elder of the Illinois Conference, is a large, fine-looking man, and he has so much the appearance of a statesman, that he is sometimes called "Sumner Brown."

BROWN, WILLIAM H., an elder in the Baltimore Conference, was born in Baltimore 1820, and was admitted into the Conference in 1866, and was transferred to the South Carolina Conference, where he did a noble work. He is now laboring in the Baltimore Conference, and is held in high esteem by his brethren.

BROWN, ANDREW, one of the oldest elders in the North Georgia Conference and the oldest P. E. in the state.

BROWN, WILLIAM H., an elder in the Pittsburg Conference, was born in Virginia, and studied awhile at Wilberforce University. He then went into the army, and on returning from there he went to Wilberforce again. He was taken from there and sent as a missionary to Kentucky. He succeeded well.

BROWN, GABRIEL P., presiding elder in the Alabama Conference, was born in the State of Georgia, entered the Conference of that state soon after its organization, and is an untiring worker.

BROWN, THOMAS H., was born a slave in the State of Maryland. He was sold South when he was a young man. He was admitted to the first Conference organized in Georgia, and he was also elected a delegate to the General Conference of 1868, held in the City of Washington. While there he visited Baltimore to see if he could find any of his relatives, but alas! they were all gone. He returned home to Georgia, and in a few years finished his course.

BROWN, E. LOUISA, the wife of Bishop Brown, was born in Louisville, Ky. She is a wife and mother in every sense of the word, raising her children in the fear of the Lord.

BROWN, GEORGE H., an elder in the Columbia Conference, is a man of industry.

BRYANT, E. M., an elder in the North Alabama Conference, was born in Alabama. He was educated at Atlanta, Ga., and is considered one of the most scholarly ministers in the Conference. He was appointed at the General Conference of 1880 editor of the *Southern Christian Recorder*. At present he is stationed at Florence, Ala.

BRYANT, HENRY E., an elder in the West Tennessee Conference, was presiding elder for several years, and represented his Conference twice in the General Conference.

BULAUGH, JEREMIAH G., an aged member of the Philadelphia Conference, was born in Delaware, taken into Conference by Bishop Allen and ordained by him. He lived to a good old age and died in Philadelphia, Pa.

BUNDY, JASON, an elder in the Indiana Conference,

was born and raised in Richmond, Ind. He was first employed by Bishop Quinn to fill a vacancy in the Conference, and was afterward admitted into the Conference. He proved himself to be a very efficient minister.

BUNDY, CHARLES, a member of the Ohio Conference, was a student at Wilberforce for a while, and entered the Conference. He has been successful as a pastor.

BURCH, CHARLES, a very able minister, was admitted into the New York Conference about 1843, and after spending some years in that Conference he was transferred to the Indiana Conference, where he labored until the Louisiana Conference was organized. He was then transferred to that Conference, where he labored and died. As a debater upon the Conference floor he had but few equals.

BURKE, MOSES, an aged minister and member of the Kentucky Conference, was born a slave, but succeeds in every charge he serves.

BURLEY, JOHN H. W., was born in Baltimore, Md., and received a common school education in that city. Afterward he went to Oberlin College, Ohio. After leaving there he was admitted into the New England Conference, and died in Washington, D. C., 1878.

BUTLER, JOHN, an elder in the Philadelphia Conference, was born in Washington City, and was recommended from Israel Church to the Philadelphia Conference. He was admitted in May 1841, and continued to labor successfully until August 1857, when he fell at his post, and his remains were brought to Washington, D. C., and there buried.

BUTLER, PATRICK, a local preacher of Philadelphia, was born in Maryland, but spent his days and labors in his adopted city.

C

CABINET (ecclesiastically speaking) refers to the bishop and presiding elders when assembled at an Annual Conference to consult and arrange the appointments of the preachers.

CAIRO, Ill., is a flourishing town on the Ohio River. It has one A. M. E. church, which was erected by Rev. Frederick Myers. It was blown down in 1879, but it has been reared again.

CALDWELL, PRINCE N., a layman, was born in Camden, Delaware, and has been a trustee and steward of the Church for years. He is a man of some means and a practical mechanic.

CALDWELL, THOMAS B., a member of the Kentucky Conference, was born in Salem, Ohio. He was a soldier in the late war. On being discharged from the army he was admitted into the Pittsburgh Conference. He spent two years at the Western Theological Seminary at Alleghany City. After leaving there, he was transferred to the Kentucky Conference and appointed to Quinn Chapel, Louisville, Ky.

CALIFORNIA CONFERENCE was organized by Bishop Campbell at San Francisco in 1865. It embraces the States of California, Oregon, Nevada, and the Territories of Washington and Utah.

CAMBRIDGE, Mass., has one A. M. E. church of about seventy-five members and a good Sunday School.

CAMBRIDGE, Md. The A. M. E. Church was organized in this town about 1818, and has come up through fire. Several of her ministers were compelled to leave, while others were put in prison. A few years ago the church was burned down, but since then another beautiful brick edifice has been erected and dedicated.

CAMDEN, N. J. The A. M. E. Church of this City was organized in the days of Bishop Allen. The membership is about two hundred. It has a large Sunday School.

CAMDEN, Delaware, is a town that has had for many years a great many members of the Society of Friends. The A. M. E. Church was organized in this town by the late Rev. Andrew Massey. Since then another A. M. E. church has been built in the eastern part of the town, called the "Star."

CAMPBELL, CATHERINE, mother of Bishop Campbell, was born in Delaware and died in Philadelphia at a good old age.

CAMPBELL, MARY A., the wife of Bishop Campbell, is an estimable Christian and a great worker for the cause of Christ.

CANNON, NOAH C. W., was born near "Cannon Ferry," Delaware. He entered the Philadelphia Conference when a young man and continued in active service until the day of his death. He filled important stations in Washington, D. C., Baltimore, Md., Philadelphia, New York and Boston. He died September 1850, sixty-four years of age, at Canonsburg, Canada, a place bearing his name.

CAPE MAY, N. J., is the great watering place, where a great many of our people spend the summer. There is one A. M. E. church in this city; membership about seventy-five.

CARR, AUGUSTUS T., a member of the South Carolina Conference, was born in Georgetown, S. C. At an early age was received into the Church and licensed to preach. At the close of the late war he welcomed the A. M. E. Church to his town, and was among the first who said, " I will go with you, for I hear the Lord is with you." He was admitted into the first Conference held in Charleston, South Carolina, and from that date to the present he has filled some of the most important positions in the Conference. He was elected to represent his Church in the Ecumenical Council at London, and while there preached to the admiration of all who heard him.

CARGILL, JOHN M., of the Baltimore Conference, was born August 30th, 1846, and admitted into the Georgia Conference January 1868. He has served several stations in the Baltimore Conference.

CARR, C., a member of the North Mississippi Conference.

CARR, SNYDER SIMON, was a worthy local preacher who lived in Hollidaysburg, Pa. for many years, and was considered by all who knew him as a man of Christian integrity. He passed away calmly, leaving a wife and several children to mourn his loss.

CARMAN, ANDREW J., a member of the Kentucky Conference, is a man of considerable promise.

CARROLL, DANIEL, an elder in the Baltimore Conference, was born in Prince George County, Md. After entering the Conference, he spent some time at the Howard University, Washington, D. C., studying theology. He is now recognized as one of the rising young ministers of the Conference.

CAREY, A. J., a member of the Georgia Conference.

CARSON, WILLIAM J., of the Texas Conference and a great frontier preacher, takes no denial, but drives ahead. He is highly appreciated by his Conference.

CARTER, DUDLEY, an aged member of the Missouri Conference, is a man of an unblemished Christian character.

CATTO, WILLIAM T., late member of the New Jersey Conference, was born in Charleston, South Carolina. He was educated by the Presbyterian Church to go as a missionary to Africa. He started, but when he got as far as Philadelphia he changed his mind and joined the Philadelphia Conference, in 1848. At the General Conference of 1852 he was elected the General Book Steward, but he resigned in a few weeks. His favorite son, Prof. Catto, was killed in Philadelphia during an election riot, which so shocked him that he broke down and never again rallied. Soon after he died.

CHAMPION, JAMES, one of the founders of the A. M.

E. Church in Philadelphia, was cotemporary with Bishop Allen, and also assisted in his ordination.

CHAMBERS, EDWARD, an elder of the Baltimore Conference, was born a slave in Baltimore, Md. He joined Bethel Church in that city when he was a young man. When Dr. Pugh, to whom he belonged, died, he was willed free. In 1850 he was received on trial in the Baltimore Conference, in which he labored faithfully, and fell at his post in Danville, Pa., sending word to his brethren that he died with the harness on.

CHAMBERS, LEWIS C., was born a slave in Cecil County, Md. He bought his freedom in 1844, and moved to Philadelphia and joined the A. M. E. Church. He then went to Canada and returned in 1868, and was admitted by transfer into the Philadelphia Conference, where he is now laboring with great success.

CHAMBERS, WILLIAM H., of the Baltimore Conference, was born in Baltimore, Maryland. He entered Lincoln University, Pennsylvania, and spent some time there. After leaving the University he was admitted to the conference, and is now one of its leading young men.

CHAMBERS, ANDREW J., at present a member of the New England Conference, was appointed by the Arkansas Conference agent for the Allen Monument. He succeeded in raising the money and the monument was erected on the Centennial grounds.

CHAMBERSBURG, Pa. The A. M. E. Church was organized in this city more than fifty years ago by some of the early pioneers. It has a membership of one hundred and fifty, a good Sunday School and a new church building.

CHAMPAIGN, Ill. There is one small church in this town with a small membership.

CHARLESTON, South Carolina, is the largest city in the state. The A. M. E. Church was reorganized in this city by the late Rev. James Lynch in 1865. There are two large churches and congregations. Emmanuel, built by Rev. Dr. Cain (now Bishop) has a membership of nearly four thousand, and Morris Brown Chapel has a membership of thirteen hundred.

CHASE, SAMUEL W., is a layman of some prominence in Bethel Church, Baltimore, Md.

CHATTANOOGA, Tenn. The A. M. E. Church was planted in this city soon after the war and has been gradually growing ever since. The membership is about two hundred.

CHESTER, Pa. The A. M. E. Church was organized in this city in 1845 by the late Rev. Stephen Smith of Philadelphia. It has a membership of about two hundred.

CHICAGO, Ill., is the great city of the North West. The A. M. E. Church has three charges in this city, viz: Quinn Chapel, Bethel and the West Side. The membership is about seven hundred.

CHILLICOTHE, Ohio. This is one of the oldest stations in the Ohio Conference, and is now one of the best points in the Conference. Rev. Jonathan B. Hamilton ended his ministerial career in this station.

CHILLICOTHE, Mo., is a small town on the Kansas Missouri Railroad. There is a small A. M. E. church there; membership about one hundred and twenty-five.

CHRISTIAN RECORDER. The organ of the A. M. E. Church. The General Conference of 1848 ordered the publication of a weekly journal called *Christian Herald*. It continued for four years under the editorial management of Rev. A. R. Green. At the General Conference of 1852 its name was changed to *Christian Recorder*, and under that name it has continued for near thirty years. It is now edited by Rev. Benjamin Tucker Tanner, D. D. There are about ten thousand copies published every week.

CINCINNATI, Ohio, is sometimes called the Queen City of the West. The A. M. E. Church has had an existence in this city for years. A few years ago the congregation sold out the old church on 6th Street and bought the large Jewish synagogue on Broadway, where they now worship. The membership is about four hundred.

CIRCLEVILLE, Ohio, a town on the Pittsburg and Cincinnati Railroad. The A. M. E. Church has existed here for years; membership two hundred.

CLARK, MOLSTON M., was born in Delaware 1807. After receiving a primary education he entered the college at Cannonburg, Pa., where he spent several years. He afterward entered the ministry of the A. M. E. Church. In 1844 he was elected the secretary of the General Conference, and was also elected traveling agent for the Book Concern. He soon resigned and went to England to attend the Evangelical Alliance. Returning from England, he was in 1852 elected the editor of the *Christian Recorder*, which position he filled a few years and resigned. A few years afterward he went to Liberia, Africa, and was principal of the Monrovia Academy. He returned to America in 1861, and resumed his former relations in the A. M. E. Church. He served acceptably the stations at New Orleans, La., and Louisville, Ky. He wound up his career at Alton, Illinois. He was considered a very able scholar and a most eloquent preacher.

CLARK, STEPHEN, was born in Prince George County, Md. He was licensed to preach in the A. M. E. Church in Washington, D. C., and was ordained a deacon by the late Bishop Waugh of that Church. In 1857 he was admitted into the Baltimore Conference of the A. M. E. Church, but served the Church only two years. While the Conference was in session in Baltimore, April 1859, he died. The whole Conference attended his funeral.

CLARK, GEORGE H., a former member of the Ohio Conference, came from Canada some years ago and joined that Conference, and after filling some prominent stations he was transferred to the South, when he ceased to work and passed away.

CLARK, REUBEN C., a young minister of the Ohio Conference, was born in Tennessee. He studied at Wilberforce, and is now filling a responsible station in the Conference.

CLARK, LEWIS D., was admitted into the North

Carolina Conference in 1870, and continued in the work until 1880, when he was overtaken by sickness, and after a few weeks his frail constitution gave way and he died surrounded by his friends and members.

CLARKSVILLE, is a beautiful town situated on the Cumberland River, Tennessee. The A. M. E. Church has occupied a conspicuous place in this town for some years. It is one of the finest stations in the West Tennessee Conference.

CLINTON, Iowa. There is a small A. M. E. Church in this town, with a fine membership and a good Sunday School.

CLEVELAND, Ohio, is one of the fine cities on the Lakes. The A. M. E. Church has a strong foothold. A year ago they sold their old house and bought another on one of the finest avenues in the city. The membership is large, and the Sunday School is in good condition.

COBURN, DANIEL, a layman in one of the churches in Baltimore, was a most excellent man. He died in 1853, leaving a large family.

COBURN, ELLEN, the wife of Daniel Coburn, was a woman of great moral worth. During her last illness she invited her friends to come and see a Christian die. She sang and clapped her hands until life's wheels stood still, and then with a sweet smile upon her face she bid children and friends adieu and went home.

. COKER, DANIEL, was one of the founders of the A. M. E. Church. He was born in Baltimore, Md., but left when he was young and went to New York, and was there educated. He returned to Baltimore, and his freedom was bought. After spending several years in the Church he went to Africa, and there died.

COLE, THOMAS M., a member of the Baltimore Conference, was born in Talbot County, Md., and admitted into the conference in 1868.

COLE, JACOB H., a late member of the Ohio Conference, was born in Chester County. He was educated at Lincoln University, Pennsylvania, and entered the Presbyterian Church. He soon left and united with the Ohio Conference. After filling several stations in that conference he finished his work at New Richmond, Ohio, 1881.

COLEMAN, L. B., of the Alabama Conference, was born 1849, and admitted into the conference in 1875.

COLEMAN, WILLIAM, H., a member of the Ohio Conference, is one of the most successful pastors in the conference. He never fails to build up the work wherever he is sent.

COLEMAN, JOHN, was born in Kentucky. After he joined the Church he spent six years at Wilberforce University. After he graduated he was admitted into the Conference, where he is operating successfully as a minister.

COLLETT, JOHN H., a young elder of the Baltimore Conference, was born in Wilmington, North Carolina. He was admitted into the North Carolina Conference and then transferred to the Baltimore Conference. He is a young man of great promise.

COLLINS, ROBERT, a local preacher, of Philadelphia, was born a slave in Maryland. He came to Baltimore, and, after he was converted, joined Bethel Church in that city. He subsequently purchased his freedom and moved to Philadelphia, where he lived until June, 1856, when he said to the writer, holding up his right hand: "I have fought a good fight," and then calmly fell asleep.

COLLINS, JOHN M., presiding elder of the White River District, Arkansas, was born September 10, 1854, in Barwell County, South Carolina. He was admitted into the Georgia Conference in 1877, and was transferred to the Arkansas Conference, where he is now laboring.

COLUMBIA, Pa., is a beautiful town, situated on the north side of the Susquehanna river. The A. M. E. Church was organized in this town by Rev. David Smith, the oldest living minister in the A. M. E. Church, and she has continued to grow until the present time.

COLUMBUS, Ga., is situated near the dividing line of Georgia and Alabama. It has two fine A. M. E. churches—St. James' and St. John's. The membership is about fifteen hundred.

COLUMBUS, Ohio, is the capital of the state. The A. M. E. Church was first organized in this city about 1823. The present St. Paul Chapel was built in 1872, and is a very fine edifice and is entirely free from debt.

CONOVER, LEWIS I., a local preacher of Freehold, New Jersey, was a man of Christian integrity and did a good work in his day.

COOK, ISAAC, an elder in the Columbia Conference, South Carolina, is a very good man.

COOK, WILLIAM, a worthy local preacher, of Washington, D. C., has been identified with the A. M. E. Church for many years. He has lived with some of the Cabinet officers of several Presidents of the United States. In these last days he has become very much afflicted, yet his mind is much composed.

COOK, E. JOHN, a member of the Virginia Conference, was born in North Carolina. He has filled important stations in his conference.

COOPER, EZEKIEL, a very excellent local deacon, lived for a great many years at Port Elizabeth, New Jersey, and was respected by all classes of citizens in the town where he lived and died. He was born a slave in Maryland, but went to New Jersey when he was a young man. It is said that his end was very peaceful.

COOPER, DANIEL, a former member of the Indiana Conference, asked for a transfer to one of the Southern conferences. His request was granted, and he entered upon his work very cheerfully; but alas! his career was short and his race soon run, and he entered the saint's rest.

COOPER, JOHN FRISBY, was born in Caroline County, Maryland, but grew up in Wilmington, Delaware, where he received a good common school education, and for several years was employed teaching school. He was admitted into the Philadelphia Conference 1867, and after spending several years in that and the New Jersey Conference, was transferred to the New England Conference and stationed at the First Church in Providence, R. I.

COOPER, PETER C., a member of the Illinois Conference, was born in Kentucky. When a young man he left his native home and went to the City of Chicago, where he joined the A. M. E. Church, and soon thereafter was admitted into the conference. He has been a great success wherever he has been stationed.

COOPER, JOHN W., a prominent member of the New Jersey Conference, was born in New York, and entered the Conference of New York when quite young, and was its secretary for several years. He was subsequently transferred to the New Jersey Conference, where he now fills an important station.

COOPER, WILLIAM G., a local deacon of Philadelphia, was born in Charleston, South Carolina. He was connected with Zion Mission Church in Philadelphia, and was much respected while living. His death was regretted by all who knew him.

COOPER, THOMAS J., late a member of the Philadelphia Conference, was born in the City of Baltimore. His father and mother were both members of the M. E. Church. He was admitted into the Conference in 1861, and soon began to rise in the estimation of his brethren. In 1864 he was appointed to that important station, Trenton, New Jersey, which was then a part of the Philadelphia Conference. In the latter part of 1865 his health began to fail. April 1866 he fell at his post in Trenton, New Jersey.

COPPIN, LEVI J., an elder in the Baltimore Conference, was born December 24, 1848. He was admitted into the Philadelphia Conference May 1877. He is now stationed in Baltimore, Md.

CORNELL, JOHN, a well-to-do layman of Georgetown, D. C., was one of the founders of the A. M. E. Church in that city.

CORNISH, WILLIAM A., late a superannuated member of the Baltimore Conference, was born in Delaware. At an early age he joined the Church, and was among some of the first recruits that Bishop Allen received after the connection was formed. After his admission into the Conference he gave signs of great strength as a preacher and debater. He filled nearly all the prominent stations, such as New York, Philadelphia, Baltimore, and Washington, D. C. He was a prominent candidate for the Episcopacy in 1836, but Edward Waters was elected over him. He took a superannuated relation in 1840, and continued therein until some time in the latter part of 1847. When he came to his end, he said to the many who called to see him, "Happy! happy! happy!"

CORNISH, JOHN, late a member of the Philadelphia Conference, was a brother of Rev. William A. Cornish. He was also born in Delaware, and early connected himself with the A. M. E. Church. He was a local preacher for some years, and was called by the Bishop to fill a vacancy on the Salem, New Jersey, Circuit as the colleague of Rev. Israel Scott. At the next conference he was admitted, and for years he filled some of the most important charges in the connection. The last one was Bethel Church, Philadelphia. He took a superannuated relation, in which he continued until June 1860, when he came to his end. A brother who spent a night with him during his illness, said he was heard to say in the stillness of the midnight hour, "My witness is in heaven, and record is on high."

CORNISH, JOHN C., a member of the New Jersey Conference, was born in Chester County, Pa., 1820. He went to Philadelphia before he was grown, and was identified with Bethel Church of that city. Some years after, he was admitted into the conference, and has been a success in every appointment assigned him.

CORR, CHARLES, an eminent local preacher of Philadelphia, was born in Charleston, South Carolina. He is spoken of as being a strong man.

CORR, JOSEPH M., an eloquent local preacher, the son of Rev. Charles Corr, was born in Charleston, South Carolina. He was licensed to preach in Philadelphia, and for years was the General Book Steward for the connection. He published the Hymn Book and Discipline which were used by the Church. He was a tailor by trade. His death was regretted by the members of other churches as well as his own.

COSBY, EDMUND, a wealthy local elder of New York, was born in Virginia. He went from his native state to New York City, and was subsequently admitted into the New York Conference, and went as a missionary to Canada and organized the Church there. On his return to New York he located. He was a man of great power in prayer, and as a preacher he was regarded as a giant.

COX, JOSEPH, a strong local elder of Philadelphia, was born in that city, and received a good common school education. He was ordained by Bishop Allen. He was no ordinary man. His sermons were clear, logical and forcible. He died in August 1843.

COX, JOHN P., was born in Frederick, Md. He was converted when quite young and joined the M. E. Church. A few years afterward he withdrew and united with the A. M. E. Church. In 1870 he was admitted into the conference, and has distinguished himself in every charge he has filled. He always builds up and never tears down.

CRAWFORD, ANDREW J., a member of the Kentucky Conference, has been presiding elder of a district and is an acceptable pastor.

CRAWFORD, SILAS, a presiding elder in the West Kentucky Conference, was born in that state, and is considered a very energetic worker.

CRIPPIN, ABRAM C., a late member of the New York Conference, was born in Drummondtown, Va., but raised in Philadelphia, and died in Trenton, 1880. He was a man of sound judgment.

CROGER, BENJAMIN and PETER, were both local deacons in Brooklyn, New York.

CROSBY, LEMUEL, a late member of the Indiana Conference, was born in the State of Michigan, where he was educated. After he was admitted he soon took the front rank in the Conference as a preacher. In 1869 he was appointed to Detroit, Mich., and during that winter, while holding a protracted meeting, he broke down and in the ensuing April died.

CROSBY, LORENZO DOW, a young member of the Indiana Conference, was born in the State of Michigan, where he attended the public school. In 1875 he was admitted into the Indiana Conference, and has been rising ever since. He is now filling one of the most prominent stations in the Conference.

CROSBY, CASSIUS M., a youthful member of the Indiana Conference, is now a student at Wilberforce University.

CORUSEY, ABRAHAM, an aged local preacher, was born in Delaware, but moved to Pennsylvania some years ago and settled in Chester County, where he now resides. He is a remarkably good man.

CUFF, A. THOMAS, a member of the Philadelphia Conference, was born in New Jersey.

CUFF, REUBEN, a local elder and one of the founders of the A. M. E. Church in Salem, New Jersey, died at a good age.

CUMBASH, JOHN W., a young member of the Philadelphia Conference, was born in Baltimore, Md., and raised in Troy, N. Y. He graduated from Wilberforce University, and is now actively engaged in the itinerancy.

CUMBERLAND, Md., is a city in the western part of

the state. The A. M. E. Church was organized in that city by Rev. Thomas W. Henry and Jacob Mitchell, and is now a fine station.

CURTIS, WILLIAM, a late member of the Indiana Conference, was considered one of the ablest scripturians in the Church. He died at Charlestown, Ind.

D

DALTON, Ga., is a beautiful town, and has one A. M. E. church with a good membership.

DANVILLE, Pa., is a town among the hills. There is a small A. M. E. church building in it, and the membership is also very small.

DANVILLE, Va., is a town on the Richmond and Danville Railroad. The A. M. E. church is the only colored Methodist church in the town. It was built by Rev. John E. Cook.

DARKS, BENJAMIN, a member of the Philadelphia Conference, was born a slave in Hagerstown, Md. He is one of the strong men of the Conference.

DAVENPORT, Iowa, is situated on the Mississippi River. The A. M. E. church was erected in this town in 1862.

DAVIDSON, H. J., a member of the Alabama Conference, was born in Alabama, November 1852, admitted into the Alabama Conference, December 1878, and is an active minister in the Conference.

DAVIDSON, WILLIAM, a venerable member of the Ohio Conference, was born in North Carolina. He emigrated to Ohio when he was a young man and settled at Oxford, Ohio. Since his admission into the Ohio Conference he has filled some important charges.

DAVIS, DANRIDGE FAYETTE, late of the Ohio Conference, was born in Kentucky, and received a good education, and was licensed to preach. It is said he had a vision one night in which he saw a large Christian army led on by a man of his own color. He inquired of some young white men who had been over in Ohio if they ever had heard of a Conference of colored men. He was told that over in Ohio the colored people had their own Bishops and Conferences, and if he would go over there in the ensuing August he would see them. He made ready and left. On reaching there, he met Bishop Morris Brown and the members of the Conference. He was introduced to them, and then and there was admitted to the Conference. After filling several important stations, he died in great peace.

DAVIS, EDWARD D., a member of the Ohio Conference, was educated at Oberlin College, Ohio, and filled some of the best charges in the Conference. While stationed in the City of Cincinnati, Ohio, in 1866, he finished his work and died with harness on, leaving a wife and several children.

DAVIS, HENRY, was born in Philadelphia, July 15th, 1819, was converted in 1830, licensed to preach in 1840 and admitted into the Philadelphia Conference in 1844. He filled several stations in the cities of Philadelphia and New York. He was a preacher of power. After spending twenty-nine years in the work, he returned to the place where he started from, viz., Burlington, N. J., and there died Jan. 17th, 1874.

DAVIS, WILLIAM, J., one of the oldest elders in the Illinois Conference, was born in Kentucky and raised by a white Christian family, who first taught him how to read. He left his native state and went to Indiana, where he joined the A. M. E. Church a few years afterward. He was admitted into the Indiana Conference and filled many of the most important stations. He was then transferred to the Illinois Conference, where he is now laboring.

DAVIS, ALEXANDER, a local preacher of Philadelphia, was born in Delaware. He spent the most of his days in his adopted city. As a preacher he was strong and eloquent. He died in 1846.

DAVIS, DENNIS, an elder of the Baltimore Conference, was born in Baltimore County, Md., and was admitted into the Baltimore Conference in 1862. His last appointment was Hagerstown, Md. In January 1864 his health failed, and he was brought home to Baltimore to die. His death was very triumphant.

DAVIS, HENDERSON, was born a slave in Prince George's County, Md. He was sold from Washington, D. C., with a large number of other slaves, and placed on board of a ship bound to some Southern port. A storm overtook her and she was driven into some English port.

The whole cargo of slaves were freed. Davis went to Frankford, Pa., and settled. He was admitted into the New York Conference in 1866. After spending a few years in that Conference, he was transferred to the Philadelphia Conference, where he is doing a good work.

DAVIS, EDWARD B., a late member of the New York Conference, was born in the State of Delaware. When a young man he went to New York to live. The first position he filled in the church after he joined was that of sexton; then he was given license as a local preacher, and was subsequently admitted into the conference, where he spent his days and died in peace.

DAVIS, JOHN W., an elder in the Philadelphia Conference, is a man of some prominence. He was formerly connected with the Zion Church, and is considered a very excellent man.

DARDIS, GEORGE, a member of the New Jersey Conference, was formerly from the M. E. Church. He is a strong preacher. He is now stationed at Salem, N, J.

DAVIS, WILLIAM H., a member of the Philadelphia Conference, is a young man of some promise, and has success in all the charges he serves.

DAWSON, JOHN B., a member of the Illinois Conference, was born in Wheeling, West Va., where he spent his youthful days. He then moved to Chicago, Ill. He is now one of the leading men of that Conference.

DAYTON, Ohio, is a great railroad centre. The A. M. E. Church has had an existence in this town for years.

DENHAM, T. C., is a presiding elder in the East Florida Conference. He is a man of promise.

DENSON, B. J., a member of the Alabama Conference.

DENTON, Md., is a town on the Choptank River. The A. M. E. Church was organized in this town about 1820, and continued to flourish until 1830, when the ministers were compelled to leave. The Church then went down. In 1868 there was another organization. The Church is now in a flourishing condition.

DENVER, Col., is a beautiful city. The A. M. E. Church has had an existence here for ten years. Here Rev. John R. V. Morgan died.

DEPUGH, HENRY, is a member of the Illinois Conference, and one of her active workers.

DERRICK, WILLIAM B., a member of the New York Conference, was born in one of the West India Islands. He was admitted into the Baltimore Conference in 1867. He now fills the Albany Station, N. Y.

DESMOND, WILLIAM, a late member of the New England Conference, died June 27, 1860.

DETROIT, Mich., is considered the largest city in the state. The A. M. E. Church has two stations in this city, viz., Bethel and Ebenezer.

DICKERSON, HENRY, an aged local deacon of Woodbury, N. J., the father of the present Bishop Dickerson, was born in Maryland and died at Woodbury, N. J. (his home), at a good age.

DICKERSON, ANNA, one of the noblest of women,

was a member of Bethel Church, Baltimore, Md, for many years. She was respected by all who knew her. She was the President of the Daughters of Conference for a long time, and died in Christ.

DICKSON, MOSES, a member of the Kansas Conference. He is a man of some ability and always succeeds.

DIGGS, JOHN W., a member of the Virginia Conference, was born in Frederick, Md. He was a soldier in the late war, and was wounded. He is now a worker for the cause.

DILLON, ISAAC, a member of the Ohio Conference, was born in Virginia, was admitted into the Conference 1857, and has continued in active work to the present.

DILLON, PHEBEA, the wife of Rev. Isaac Dillon, was a most excellent woman, and greatly assisted her husband in his work in all the charges he filled. Her death was just such an one as would be expected.

DIXON, H. E., a member of the Alabama Conference, was born in Lafayette, Ala., June 7, 1848. He was admitted into the Alabama Conference in 1874, and has continued to grow gradually ever since. He is considered the ablest financier in the Conference.

DOBSON, PERRY, ABRAM and WILLIAM, were all brothers and local preachers in the A. M. E. Church. They were born in Easton, Md. They were regarded as good men.

DOBSON, CHARLES, a local deacon of Easton, Md., was the son of William Dobson. He died a few years since.

DORSEY, JOHN W., is a member of the Kansas Conference.

DORRELL, DEATON, was a prominent member of the New York Conference for more than thirty years, and was regarded as one of the leading members of his Conference. At four successive General Conferences he was Chairman of the Committee on Episcopacy. In 1880 he was appointed to Albany City Station. He went to his work cheerfully and was beloved by all. He retired on Saturday night in his usual health. Sunday morning came, the congregation gathered; but the pastor not making his appearance, the door of the parsonage was broken open, and there was Rev. Deaton Dorrell cold in death. He was taken home to Brooklyn to his family and there buried.

DOVE, WILLIAM A., a member of the Missouri Conference, was born in Westchester, Pa., and was raised in Boston, where he was licensed to preach. In 1848 he started for the West, and was admitted into the Indiana Conference, where he labored some years successfully. He is considered a great disciplinarian and an able preacher.

DRAPER, DANIEL, a member of the Baltimore Conference, was born in Baltimore City, and learned the trade of a barber. He was admitted into the Baltimore Conference in 1864, and has continued to occupy conspicuous places in the Conference until the present.

DRAYTON, SAMUEL W., a member of the Georgia Conference. He was an elder in the M. P. Church before the war. He joined the A. M. E. Church as soon as it was organized in the state. He is now a presiding elder in his Conference.

DUNN, CHARLES, a man of precious memory, was a local deacon in Bethel Church, Baltimore, Md. He was known wherever he went as Father Dunn, and he was loved by all who knew him. He was also called the sweet singer. He occupied a chair in the altar, and before it was time for service to commence he would sing one or two of his favorite songs. One was, "Come, brothers and sisters, that love one another." In the summer of 1863 he left the shores of time.

DUNN, MARY, the wife of Rev. Charles Dunn, was a remarkable Christian woman, and greatly assisted her husband in the ministry. Her end was sudden, and yet peaceful.

DUNLOP, GEORGE W., a layman and a man of some means, was born in Prince George's County, Md., and, after living there for years, moved to Washington, D. C., and joined old Israel Church. Being a good writer, he was elected the recording steward for the church, which position he occupied until the day of his death. In August 1858 he closed his eyes in death.

E

EADDIS, W. JOHN, a member of the Illinois Conference, was born in Kentucky and raised by Dr. Dandy, of the M. E. Church. He is an eloquent preacher.

EARLEY, JORDAN W., one of the fathers and founders of the Tennessee Conference, was born in Virginia. He moved to St. Louis, Mo., in his youth, and commenced business and accumulated considerable. He was one of the founders of the A. M. E. Church of the City of St. Louis, Mo. He is considered one of the best pastors and managers of a church in the Conference, and for years led the ticket for delegates to the General Conference.

EARLEY, SARAH E., the wife of Rev. J. W. Earley, is a highly educated Christian lady and excellent teacher, and has done much to lift up the down-trodden.

EASTON, Md., is a beautiful town in Talbot County. The A. M. E. Church was first organized in this town by the late Rev. Shadrach Bassett. Joseph Chain and Washington Dorrell—both local preachers—were the two men who aided in the work. The Baltimore Conference has held two sessions in this town.

EDDY, JOSHUA P. B., one of the oldest local elders in Philadelphia, was born in the western part of Pennsylvania. He was admitted into the Philadelphia Conference when he was a young man, was ordained deacon and elder by Bishop Allen, and also married his (Allen's) daughter. He afterward located and now lives in Philadelphia. He is regarded as one of the wealthiest men of color in that city.

EDDY, JOSIAH, a local deacon of Philadelphia and brother of Rev. Joshua P. B. Eddy, has been a member and minister in Bethel Church, Philadelphia, for some years.

EDWARDS, SAMUEL, a local deacon of New York,

was a man to be relied on. He was the elder's armor-bearer. He was a local delegate to the General Conference of 1840. He died several years ago in the City of New York.

EDWARDS, HARDY D., an influential member of the South Carolina Conference, was among the first who were admitted into the Conference after its organization, and filled some of the most responsible stations in the Conference. He died in 1880. The vacancy caused by his death will be hard to fill for some time.

ELZYMORE, JOHN, an elder in the New England Conference, served the Church very acceptably for years and died Dec. 16, 1865.

EMBRY, JAMES C., an eminent elder of the Kansas Conference, was born in Illinois. He has a respectable education. At one time he was the commissioner of Education, and subsequently he was chosen Financial Secretary, and filled both positions with great credit to himself and satisfaction to the connection. At the General Conference of 1881 he was chosen one of the delegates to the Ecumenical Council at London.

EMORY, ISAAC, a local deacon of Providence, R. I., was born in Salem, New Jersey.

EUFAULA, Ala., is a handsome town. The A. M. E. Church was organized in this place soon after the war, and is one of the finest stations in the state. Membership about four hundred.

EVANS, JAMES, was a local elder. He lived in Alexandria, Va., for many years, and then moved to Columbus, Ohio, and there died.

EVANS, ROBERT, a local deacon of Bordentown, New Jersey, was a man of Christian integrity. He was ordained by Bishop Morris Brown and died in 1866.

EVANS, RACHEL, the wife of Rev. Robert Evans, was a preacheress of no ordinary ability. She could rouse a congregation at any time, and was a woman of unblemished Christian character. They raised a family of Christian children. They both sleep side by side in the graveyard awaiting the resurrection morn.

EVANS, LEVI, a venerable member of the Kentucky Conference, was born in Washington, D. C. He went to Kentucky when he was quite young, joined the Conference and filled many stations of importance.

EVANSVILLE, Ind., is a city situated on the north side of the Ohio River. The A. M. E. Church has existed here for some years. The present membership is about two hundred.

F

FARRIS, EDWARD M., of the Philadelphia Conference, was born in Philadelphia. He learned the trade of a barber, and entered the Church in his youth. He was afterwards licensed to preach, and after being ordained a deacon was admitted into the Philadelphia Conference. The first circuit he traveled was Salem, New Jersey. The next year he was changed to Bucks County, Pa. In attempting to cross a certain stream of water one cold day, he fell in and got very wet, which gave him such a cold that it brought on consumption, which caused his death.

FAUSSETT, REDMAN B., a presiding elder of the New Jersey Conference, was admitted into the Philadelphia Conference in 1867, and has since filled some of the most important stations in the Conference.

FELTS, C. C., a member of the Philadelphia Conference, was born in Virginia. He was admitted into the Ohio Conference, and then spent some time at Wilberforce University. He was subsequently transferred to the Philadelphia Conference. His first appointment was West Philadelphia. From there he was sent to Wilmington, Del., where he erected the finest church building in the state belonging to the A. M. E. Church.

FERGUSON, SAMUEL, was a leader in Bethel Church, Baltimore, Md. He went to the war in 1864, and was captured at the battle of Petersburg and taken to some of the Southern prisons, and there died.

FIELDS, ABRAM, was born in Elkton, Md., and went to Philadelphia when he was a young man. For years he was the steward of Bethel Church. He was a man of a brilliant intellect, and was very much missed when he was called away by death.

FITZHUGH, CHARLES WESLEY, an elder in the Baltimore Conference, was born in Natchez, Miss., November 12, 1842. He is now stationed in the City of Baltimore, Md.

FITZPATRICK, I. N., is a member of the Alabama Conference. He represented his Conference in the last General Conference, 1880.

FLORIDA ANNUAL CONFERENCE of the A. M. E. Church was organized June 8, 1867, in the City of Tallahassee. Its boundaries were then the whole state. The Conference since then has been divided into two—Florida and West Florida.

FLUSHING, N. Y., is one of the oldest charges on Long Island, and has a membership of one hundred and twenty-five.

FORTIE, JOHN C., an educated young layman of Baltimore, Md., member and steward of Bethel Church, died in the prime of life.

FORT SCOTT, Kansas. The A. M. E. Church was here organized in 1866, and a small building was erected. It has since been rebuilt and dedicated in 1875.

FRANKFORT, Ky., is the capital of the state. The A. M. E. Church is the only colored Methodist Church in the city, and has a membership of about two hundred and fifty, and a large Sunday School.

FREDERICK, Md., is one of the oldest stations in the state outside of Baltimore. The church was rebuilt in 1855, and remodeled in 1870. It is now one of the best stations in Western Maryland.

FREEMAN, MOSES, was one of the first ministers that was stationed in Baltimore after the organization of the Conference. His stay in Baltimore was short. He was recalled by the Bishop and sent on a foreign mission, where he died.

FREEMAN, WALLER, a layman of Union Bethel Church, Washington, D. C., was born a slave in Raleigh, N. C. His wife belonged to Hon. Mr. Badger. When General Harrison took his seat as President of the United States, Mr. Badger was invited to a seat in his Cabinet. He accepted and moved to Washington, D. C., and brought the family of Waller Freeman with him. After the death of President Harrison, Mr. Badger returned home to North Carolina. Waller Freeman, not wishing to return, was compelled to buy his whole family. They settled in Washington, D. C. They raised an interesting family of children. Waller Freeman and his wife, Eliza, have both passed away to their eternal rest.

FRY, G. G., a member of the North Carolina Conference, was born in Frankford, Pa. He has been secretary of the Conference for some time, and is considered one of the ablest ministers in the Conference.

G

GAINES, CAUSMAN H., a son of the late Rev. William Gaines of the Baltimore Conference, a worthy layman of Bethel Church, Baltimore, is a fine scholar and was for many years recording steward of the church. He is a good business man and superintendent of the "Ship Yard Company" in Baltimore. He served one term on the Grand Jury of the United States Court.

GAINES, GEORGE WASHINGTON, a member of the

Missouri Conference, was born a slave in Missouri. He went into the army, and there he began to educate himself, and when he returned he had advanced considerably. On entering the Conference he took a stand in favor of education, and is now considered one of the most progressive members of the Conference.

GAINES, WESLEY C., a member of the Georgia Conference, is a relative of the family of Gaines above referred to. He is a minister very much respected by his Conference, and was a delegate to the General Conference of 1880. He at present fills a popular station in the Conference.

GAINES, WILLIAM, once a member of the Baltimore Conference, was born on the Eastern Shore of Maryland. Coming to Baltimore, he joined Ebenezer Church. In 1843 he was admitted to the Baltimore Conference and ordained a deacon. In 1845 he was appointed to the Hagerstown Circuit, Md. Being a very industrious man, he left his family in the care of the Great Shepherd and started for his work, and had gone several rounds, when on returning to Hagerstown he was seized with something like the vertigo and fell from his horse. When found he was speechless and so remained until his death. He was buried in the old church-yard in Hagerstown. His funeral sermon was preached by his friend, Rev. Thomas W. Henry.

GAINES, WILLIAM, late of the Georgia Conference, was born a slave in Georgia. Soon after the close of the war he united with the A. M. E. Church, and was admitted into the Conference and ordained. But his ministerial career was short. He died in Georgia.

GAINES, W. J., a prominent member of the North Georgia Conference, was born a slave in Georgia and belonged to General Toombs. Soon after the war he joined the A. M. E. Church and was among the first to unite with the Conference when it was organized, and has filled nearly all the prominent appointments in the Conference. He has also represented his Conference in every General Conference since he has been eligible. On a visit once to Boston he called the roll of his former master's slaves at Bunker Hill.

GALE, GEORGE C., a layman of Bethel Church, Baltimore, Md., at one time was a trustee of the church. In 1881 he went to Rockville to do some carpenter's work for a friend of his. He was taken sick there, and before he could be brought home he died. He said to his friends before he died, "I am clinging to the Cross."

GALENA, Ill. The A. M. E. Church has a small membership in this town.

GALESBURG, Ill. The A. M. E. Church has a flourishing church and a large membership in this city.

GALLIPOLIS, Ohio, situated on the west side of the Ohio River, is one of the oldest appointments in that part of the state. The A. M. E. Church has a membership of two hundred.

GALVESTON, Texas. The A. M. E. Church is well represented in this city, and has a fine church and congregation.

GANT, N. T., a wealthy layman of Zanesville, Ohio, was elected a delegate to the Ecumenical Conference at London.

GARDNER, LAZARUS, a member of the Louisiana Conference, was formerly a member of the Georgia Conference. He was a delegate from the Georgia Conference to the General Conference of 1876, and also from the Louisiana Conference to the General Conference of 1880.

GARDNER, PETER, late of the Philadelphia Conference, was in the first part of his ministry connected with the M. E. Church. About 1847 he joined the A. M. E. Church in the West. He was then transferred to the New York Conference and was stationed at Brooklyn, New York. From there he went to the Philadelphia Conference, where he ended his days. His last illness was remarkable. He had purchased a house at Burlington, New Jersey, and when he and his Christian wife reached there, she remarked to a friend, "Now we have come here, I expect, to die." The friend said, "Well, Sister Gardner, you must try and get ready." Brother Gardner, who was sitting at the table eating milk and bread, looked up and said, "I have not got to get ready, for I am ready now." He continued to grow weaker, and one morning, when the doctor came in to see him, he said, "Doctor, I am dying, ain't I?" The Doctor said, "Yes, but you may outlive me." He said, "Yes, but I reason philosophically; if a man cannot eat he can't live." Then he said, "I have got religion, thank God! I am not afraid to die." He asked some friends to assist him up stairs, and when they reached the room he could not walk, and being heavy they could not carry him. He then told them to push him like a log. The struggle fatigued him very much. He called his wife, saying, "Serona!" She said, "What is it, husband?" "Worse and worse." That night he dreamed he was dead. The next morning his wife called him and asked what he would have for breakfast. He answered by saying, "I am dead. I cannot eat." Some one asked him how he felt when he conceived the idea he was dead. He said, "I did not feel as happy as I wanted to, for I wanted to feel that I had overcome by the blood of the Lamb." Whilst lying upon his bed he said to some friends, "I have heard it said that if you would straighten out a dying man, he would soon be gone." Then he said, "Straighten me out." The friend was slow to move, and so he said, "Did you hear?" The answer was "Yes." Then he said, "Be about it." It was done as he said, and in a few minutes he was gone.

GARDNER, PRINCE, a presiding elder of the North Alabama Conference, is a very active minister, and one of the most acceptable presiding officers in the Conference.

GASAWAY, RICHARD J., a member of the Virginia Conference, was born in Maryland, July 10, 1825, and was admitted into the Conference April 1869. Since then he has worked in Virginia.

GAZAWAY, JOHN W., a member of the Ohio Conference, was born in Ohio. He is regarded as an excellent Christian man. Success attends his labors.

GENERAL CONFERENCE of the A. M. E. Church is the highest body. It meets once in every four years on the first Monday in May.

GEORGETOWN, D. C. The A. M. E. Church was organized here in 1842, and it is a fine station, having a membership of two hundred.

GEORGIA CONFERENCE of the A. M. E. Church was organized in the city of Macon, May 30, 1867. Its boundaries then included the whole state, but since then it has been divided into two conferences, the Georgia and the North Georgia.

GIBBS, RICHARD P., was born in Kent County, Delaware. His father taught him to read and write. He was admitted into the Baltimore Conference in 1858. He filled New York City Station and Union Church, Philadelphia. From the latter place he was transferred to Savannah, Georgia, where he spent a short time, and then died, and was brought to Philadelphia and buried from the Union Church, where he was once pastor.

GIBBS, STEPHEN, a worthy layman, was born in Delaware, and was a very successful farmer and owned considerable land in the state, and died at a good old age.

GILBERT, JOSHUA, a very eloquent local preacher, was born in Harford County, Md., March 5, 1807. He went to Baltimore when a young man and was received into Bethel Church. Soon after he was licensed to preach, and very soon became the centre of attraction. Whenever it was known that he was to preach, crowds would gather.

But his brilliant career was short. His sun set without a cloud ; and so, although dead, he yet lives in the minds of the old members of the Church. He died February 24, 1838.

GILBERT, PACA THOMAS, was born in Harford County, Md., October 8, 1805. He went to Baltimore when a young man, was admitted into Bethel Church and was licensed to exhort. He was the first man that organized a Sunday School in Bethel Church, Baltimore, Md.

GLOVER, GEORGE, is one of the first laymen of the A. M. E. Church in Port Deposit, Md.

GOLDEN, JEFFERY, a very worthy member of the Baltimore Conference, was born in Baltimore City. He was a man of no learning, and yet was a remarkable preacher. He traveled circuits for several years and finally obtained a superannuated relation. He died in Baltimore, 1852.

GOODLOW, JOHN M., a presiding elder of the North Alabama Conference, was formerly a minister in the M. E. Church, but now is a very efficient worker in the Conference.

GOOSLEY, C. S., a member of the New England Conference, was formerly a member of the British M. E. Church in Canada. Some years ago he obtained a transfer to the South Carolina Conference, where he served acceptably as pastor and presiding elder. He was a member of the last General Conference.

GORDON, B. H., is a member of the Indiana Conference.

GORDON, HENRY, an excellent layman of Philadelphia, was for years the leader of the choir and also a leader and steward. When he died he left the Church and the publication department a handsome sum.

GOULD, FURMAN, a local preacher of New Jersey, was one of the great supporters of the A. M. E. Church in that part of New Jersey. He was married four times and raised a large family of children, who are either members of or friends of the Church of his choice.

GOULD, JESSE, is an excellent steward and leader in the A. M. E. Church in Gouldtown, New Jersey.

GOULD, THEODORE, a member of the Philadelphia Conference, was born in Gouldtown, New Jersey. In 1846 the minister in charge of the circuit was holding a quarterly meeting at that place and preached from the text, "Come thou and thy house into the ark." He invited any who might want to get out of the storm to come in. The first one was Theodore Gould, then a little flaxy-headed boy. The minister, laying his hand upon his head, said, "God bless this little boy."

GRAHAM, GRAFTON H., was born in New Market, Frederick County, Md. He learned the barber's trade when a youth, and then went to Allegheny City, Pa., and entered the ministry of the Zion Church and for some time attended the Avery College of that city. In 1854 he joined the A. M. E. Church, and since then has filled some of the prominent charges in the Ohio as well as in the Kentucky Conference. At present he is stationed at Middleport, Ohio, and is decidedly one of the most eloquent pulpit orators in the connection.

GRANT, ABRAHAM, of the West Texas Conference, was born in Florida and was admitted into that conference soon after it was organized. He has since been transferred to the West Texas Conference. He was a member of the General Conference of 1880.

GRAY, JOHN H. T., a member of the Baltimore Conference, has charge at present of the Quaker Bottom Circuit. He studied theology at the Howard University, and is one of the young giants of the Conference.

GREEN, ALFRED M., the son of the Rev. A. R. Green, was born in Pennsylvania. After receiving his education he devoted his time to lecturing, and then entered the army. After leaving the army he entered the ministry, was received into the Baltimore Conference, and transferred to the Louisiana Conference and stationed in New Orleans. He was a member of the General Conference of 1880.

GREEN, AUGUSTUS R., was born in Virginia. His father moved to Pennsylvania when his son was a small boy. He received a good English education, and then learned the trade of a blacksmith. In 1841 he was admitted into the Ohio Conference and soon began to rise in the estimation of the members. In 1848 the General Conference elected him the General Book Steward and editor of the "Christian Herald." He ran the concern for four years and then resigned, and returned to the pastorate and remained therein until 1860, when he removed to Canada.

When the unfortunate separation took place, he was elected the Bishop of one party, and continued to act in that capacity for several years. In 1876 he resigned his episcopal office and returned to the bosom of the A. M. E. Church, and was appointed to Vicksburg, Miss. There he labored; there he fell at his post during the yellow fever. As a preacher he was able, as a debater he was strong, as a Christian he was exemplary.

GREEN, BEDFORD, of the Tennessee Conference, was born a slave in that state. After he obtained his freedom he began to study hard and soon became one of the strong men of the Conference. He is now filling one of the largest stations in the Conference — St. Paul's Chapel, City of Nashville.

GREEN, CHARLES E., a member of the New Jersey Conference, was born in Maryland. He was admitted into the New York Conference in 1865. He is now stationed at Washington, New Jersey.

GREEN, CHARLES H., a member of the New Jersey Conference, and stationed at present in Burlington, New Jersey, is a great financier.

GREEN, CHARLES R., a member of the Ohio Conference, was born in New Jersey. He was admitted into the Ohio Conference in 1866.

GREEN, PLATO H., a son of Thomas E. Green, is a member of the Baltimore Conference.

GREEN, P. R., one of the oldest ministers in the California Conference, went to that state before there was any conference, and helped to organize and assisted in building up the Church on that coast.

GREEN, THOMAS, a local deacon in the Church at Providence, R. I., has been regarded as an upright Christian man.

GREEN, THOMAS E., a local preacher of the City of Washington, and a man of large business capacity, has done a great deal for the Church. He was lay delegate to the General Conference of 1880.

GREENLY, GEORGE, a member of the Philadelphia Conference, was born in Pennsylvania. He was admitted into the Philadelphia Conference in 1841, and spent several years in the work. His end was peaceful.

GROSS, LEVIN, was born in Maryland and for many years was a member and minister of the M. E. Church. On moving West he entered the ministry of the A. M. E. Church, and for years marched in front of the host of the Ohio Conference, and finally entered his glorious rest.

GUTRIDGE, WILLIAM, a local deacon of Washington, D. C., was born in Prince George County, Md. He was ordained in 1868 and died in 1870 in Washington, D. C.

H

HACKETT, GEORGE A., of Baltimore, Md., was a lay member of Bethel Church. No man of color was better known than he, and no man did more for his race. He was fearless in helping his people when they were in trouble.

He was chosen the chief marshal on the occasion of the celebration of the emancipation of the state of Maryland, and admirably performed his duty. He died in April, 1870. No man is more missed in Baltimore City than George A. Hackett.

HAGERSTOWN, Md., is a beautiful town situated in the mountains of Western Maryland. The A. M. E. Church was organized in this town soon after the formation of the connection, and has continued to be the leading colored Methodist church in the town. Its membership is about one hundred and seventy-five, and its Sunday School good.

HALL, ABRAM T., one of the oldest ministers in the Illinois Conference, was born in Pennsylvania. After he was admitted into the Indiana Conference he filled nearly all the popular charges, and now he is stationed in the City of Chicago.

HALL, ALBERT, a class leader in the Union Church of Philadelphia, was born in Maryland. He is regarded by all who know him as a man of moral worth.

HALL, CALEB, a local deacon, lived all his days at the place called Ellicott's Mills, and died in 1863.

HALL, ELI N., was a member of the New York Conference for years. He was born in Norfolk, Virginia, and removed to Brooklyn, New York. After spending a good many years in the itinerant work, he located and returned to his native home (Virginia) and there died.

HALL, MORRIS, a most excellent layman of Philadelphia, a member of Bethel Church, lived in one Quaker family for about forty years. When he died a large number of the Friends attended his funeral.

HALL, RICHARD A., a member of the Georgia Conference, was born in Frederick County, Md. He was converted in his youth and joined the M. E. Church, and was ordained a deacon by Bishop Janes. In 1862 he was admitted into the Baltimore Conference of the A. M. E. Church. He remained in that conference until 1877, when he was transferred to the Georgia Conference, where he is now filling a prominent station.

HALL, THOMAS, a venerable local preacher of Baltimore, Md., and a member of Bethel Church, was respected by all who knew him for his upright Christian character. He died at a good old age.

HAMILTON, ——, the mother of Lewis and D. P. Hamilton, was at the time of her death the oldest female member of Bethel Church, Wilmington, Delaware. The day she was a hundred years old she desired to be taken to the church to celebrate it there. The members looked with some interest to see the mother of the church out on that day. She then and there bid the church adieu and returned home, and in attempting to come down stairs fell and expired by the time the family reached her.

HAMILTON, DANIEL P., a layman of Bethel Church, Wilmington, Delaware, was one of the founders of the Church in that city and marched in front of the army for years, and is still leading them on. He is a man that the citizens highly respect.

HAMILTON, JESSE C., a member of the N. E. Texas Conference, was born a slave in Tennessee and sold from there further south; thence he made his way to California, and there entered the conference and labored successfully until he was transferred to the conference where he is now at work.

HAMILTON, JONATHAN B., a late member of the Ohio Conference, was born in Leesburg, Va. He left there when quite young and went north about 1857, and was admitted into the New York Conference. He subsequently worked in the Philadelphia, Georgia, Virginia and Baltimore Conferences. In 1877 he was transferred to the Ohio Conference and stationed at Chillicothe, Ohio, where he labored but a few months and then passed away. He was taken to Leesburg, Va., and there interred.

HAMILTON, LEWIS, a well-to-do layman, is a member of the church at Smyrna, Del.

HAMILTON, PATRICK, an aged local minister, was ordained by Bishop J. O. Andrew of the M. E. Church and admitted into the A. M. E. Church in 1846, and died in Baltimore, Md.

HAMMITT, EMANUEL, is a member of the West Texas Conference. As a minister he stands well in the conference, and was a member of the General Conference of 1880.

HAMMOND, SOUTHY, a venerable local preacher of Baltimore, was born in Eastern Virginia. He came to Baltimore and settled and raised a family of children. All the week he would work at his trade, shoemaking, and then on Sunday walk eight and ten miles in the country to preach. A brother who went to see him when he was dying said he asked Brother Hammond how it was with him, and he, being unable to speak, made a straight mark with his finger to indicate that his way was straight. He then folded up his arms and departed in peace.

HANCOCK, BROKER, is a member of the West Texas Conference, and was a member of the General Conference of 1880.

HANDY, ISHMAEL, a brilliant young local preacher of Baltimore, Md., was a local delegate to the General Conference of 1852, which met in New York City. His career as a preacher was short, but his end was glorious.

HANDY, JAMES A., a presiding elder in the Baltimore Conference, was born Dec. 22, 1826, and raised in Baltimore City. He showed signs of future usefulness when in his youth, and was a great debater in the lyceums and other societies. He was not converted until he was married and had a family. Then he joined the Bethel Church in Baltimore, Md. Having a business turn of mind he was very soon elected a trustee of the church, and licensed to preach. In 1862 he was admitted into the Baltimore Conference, and although but a licentiate was appointed to one of the best stations in the Conference. In 1864 he was appointed to Portsmouth, Va., and from there to Wilmington, N. C. He subsequently returned to the Baltimore Conference. In 1868 he was elected by the General Conference

Secretary of the Missionary Society of the A. M. E. Church, and has been a member of every General Conference since he has been eligible. At the General Conferences of 1876 and 1880 he was a member of the Committee on Episcopacy and acted as secretary.

HANNIBAL, Missouri, is a fine city situated on the west side of the Mississippi River. The A. M. E. Church was organized in this city in 1865, and is one of the most interesting stations in the conference.

HARMON, WILLIAM, was at the time of his death a member of the New York Conference.

HARPER, JAMES, an esteemed member of the Philadelphia Conference, was regarded as a man of solid piety. He died about middle age, beloved by the members and ministers.

HARPER, R., a member of the Tennessee Conference, was born in one of the New England States, where he was also educated. He afterwards went to Georgia and for several years filled important charges in that conference, serving as their secretary. He was also a member of the General Conference of 1880.

HARRIS, CHARLES E., the secretary of the North Alabama Conference, was born in Maryland. After he grew up to be a man he went into the army, and on leaving that entered Lincoln University and completed his course of study there. He then entered the Law School at Howard University, and thence went to Selma, Ala., where he was admitted to the bar. He represented his county in the state legislature and was subsequently admitted into the conference, in which he has been a very successful pastor.

HARRIS, CHARLES L., a leading member of the Alabama Conference, was born August 1, 1847, admitted into the Mississippi Conference in 1872, and is now the State Missionary for the whole state of Alabama.

HAWKINS. JAMES EDWARD, was born in Cecil County, Md., was admitted into the Philadelphia Conference in 1848, and transferred to the Baltimore Conference. He labored a few years, but his health failed and so he returned to Philadelphia. Then, after resting a few years, he commenced work again, but soon had to give it up. He died resting upon the promises of God.

HAYNES, JAMES E., a member of the South Carolina Conference, was born in South Carolina, was educated at Howard University, and is now a presiding elder in his conference. He was also a member of the General Conference of 1880.

HAYNES, JAMES H.. a member of the Virginia Conference, was admitted into the Baltimore Conference in 1872, and then transferred to the Virginia Conference, where he has labored successfully ever since.

HELENA, Arkansas. The A. M. E. Church in this city has about two hundred members and good church property.

HENDERSON, JESSE, a member of the Ohio Conference, was at one time a minister in the Wesley Church. He entered the Ohio Conference of the A. M. E. Church and has filled prominent stations.

HENDERSON, THOMAS WELLINGTON, a prominent member of the Missouri Conference, was born in North Carolina, and was educated at Oberlin College, Ohio. Afterwards he entered the Missouri Conference, where he has done a grand work.

HENRY, GEORGE, a layman in Bethel Church, Philadelphia, for many years was a leader and trustee. He was respected by all who knew him.

HENRY, JOHN R., a member of the Baltimore Conference, a son of the late Rev. Thomas W. Henry, was born in Hagerstown, Md. In 1860 he was admitted into the Baltimore Conference, and since then has filled important charges in the Conference.

HENRY, THEODORE A. V., a member of the Baltimore Conference, was born in Dorchester County, Md., and was admitted from the Colored Methodist Protestant Church in 1877. He is a very active worker.

HENRY, THOMAS W., at the time of his death was the oldest elder in the Baltimore Conference. He was born at Leonardtown, Md. Being a slave, he was brought from there to Hagerstown, Md., where he was converted and licensed to preach. For several years he was an acceptable local preacher in the M. E. Church, but afterwards united with the A. M. E. Church, and for thirty years was considered one of the strongest men in the Conference. In 1859 he had to leave the state of Maryland because his name was found upon some of John Brown's papers. After the war he returned home to his old Conference in April, 1877. He died in Washington, D. C., and was taken to Hagerstown, Md., and there buried.

HENRY WILLIAM, a local deacon of West Chester, Pa., was one of the founders of the A. M. E. Church in that part of the state, and in her lived and died.

HENSON, AMOS, is a useful local preacher of Bethel Church, Baltimore, Md.

HENSON, JAMES, D., is a layman of Bethel Church, Baltimore, Md., and has been a leader and trustee for several years.

HENSON, JOHN H., a late member of the Philadelphia Conference, was born a slave in Queen Anne's County, Md., but left there when a young man and went to Reading, Pa., where he joined the A. M. E. Church. In 1848 he was admitted to the Philadelphia Conference and spent the remnant of his days in the work. He died at Frankford, Pa.

HERBERT, CHARLES EDWARD, of the Philadelphia Conference, the son of Rev. John J. Herbert, was born in Hagerstown, Md. He graduated from Wilberforce University, and was then admitted to the Ohio Conference. Since then he has labored in the Kentucky and Pittsburg Conferences, and is now in the Philadelphia Conference.

HERBERT, JOHN J., a member of the Baltimore Conference, was born in Maryland and admitted to the Conference in 1848, in which he has since filled important charges.

HERROD, WILLIAM H., a member of the Kansas Conference, was born in Philadelphia. He left there and went to Missouri. In 1868 he was admitted into the conference and has filled prominent positions.

HICKS, CHARLES, a local deacon of Washington, D. C. He is regarded as a man of Christian integrity.

HICKS, GEORGE, an excellent local preacher of Washington, D. C., was a man without education; yet it is said that he as a preacher had few equals. He spent his days in Washington, and left behind him a name worthy of a minister of the Gospel.

HILL, AARON, is a member of the West Tennessee Conference, and is at present stationed at Memphis City.

HILL, ANN, the wife of Pippin Hill, was a remarkable Christian woman. After she had grown old she went to Africa, spent some time there and then came home to America and died.

HILL, BENJAMIN, a late member of the Indiana Conference, was a man without learning; yet it is said he could take up the hymn book, call the page and line the verses; and then open the Bible and call the text. He was regarded by all who knew him as a man of Christian integrity. He died some years since.

HILL, ISAAC J., a member of the New Jersey Conference, was born in Pennsylvania. He served several years in the Philadelphia Conference, and then went south and was re-admitted into the Virginia Conference, where he did a grand work. He is still in the active service.

HILL, PIPPIN, a worthy layman of Bethel Church, Baltimore, was for many years the faithful sexton of the church.

HILL, STEPHEN, a layman of the church in Baltimore, Md., was a lay delegate to the Convention of 1816 that organized the A. M. E. Church, and rendered great service. He was a man of some mental power and lived and died in the Church.

HILLERY, LEWIS, a presiding elder of the Alabama Conference, was a member of the General Conference of 1880.

HILLSBOROUGH, N. C. The A. M. E. Church was organized in this town soon after the war, and is doing well.

HILLSBOROUGH, Ohio. The A. M. E. Church has had an existence in this town for years, but never accomplished much until the last few years, when a new fine brick building was erected.

HILLSDALE, D. C., is a small town across the eastern branch of the Potomac River. There is a small church and society here.

HOGRATH, GEORGE, late General Book Steward of the A. M. E. Church, was born in Annapolis, Md. He received a good English education and for several years was the general book steward and editor of the Monthly Magazine. He died in Brooklyn, N. Y., 1850.

HOLCOME, ROBERT, a local preacher of Philadelphia, Pa., was a man that was much respected in his day for his uprightness as a Christian minister. He has long since gone to his reward.

HOLCOME, SHEPHERD, was born in Princeton, N. J., and was admitted into the Philadelphia Conference in

1848 and continued to labor for several years; but finally his health broke down and he had to retire. He died at Mount Holly, N. J.

HOLLEN, JAMES, a superannuated minister of the Philadelphia Conference, is at present the oldest man in the Conference. He has stood at his post for thirty years. At the last session of the Conference, 1881, he asked for and obtained his present relation.

HOLMES, E. P., a member of the Georgia Conference, has been a presiding elder for some time, and now is pastor of one of the finest charges in the Conference. He was a delegate to the General Conference of 1881.

HOOPER, JOHN, was a most exellent local preacher, who lived for many years in Chester County, Pa. He died and was buried there.

HOPKINS, WILLIAM HENRY, of the Philadelphia Conference, was born in Easton, Md. He was admitted into the Baltimore Conference in 1854, and continued therein until he fell into the Philadelphia Conference by the General Conference taking a certain part of Pennsylvania from the Baltimore Conference and placing it in the Philadelphia Conference. He has filled circuits and stations to the satisfaction of the people.

HOUSTON, Texas. The A. M. E. Church was organized in this city soon after the war, and is reported to be in a good condition.

HOWARD, ROBERT W., a member of the Alabama Conference, was born in Columbus, Ga., Jan. 16, 1842, and admitted into the Conference 1874.

HUBBARD, JAMES HENRY, a member of the Kansas Conference, was born in Baltimore, Md., and educated at Allegheny City, Pa. He went to California when he was quite young, and was there admitted into the California Conference. He was transferred to Missouri Conference in 1873. Since the division of the Conference he has been in the Kansas Conference.

HUBBARD, JOHN HENRY, a late member of the Missouri Conference, was born a slave in Columbia, Mo. After he was admitted into the Conference he filled some of the best appointments in the Conference. But his ministerial career was short. He departed in peace.

HUBBARD, PHILIP ALEXANDER, a member of the Kansas Conference, was born a slave in Missouri. He was admitted into the Missouri Conference in 1873. He is one of the greatest workers in the Conference, and has never failed at any point to which he has been sent.

HUDSON, MARY JANE, a member of Bethel Church, Baltimore, was for many years one of the most active workers in the church and died beloved by all who knew her.

HUGHES, JOSIAH H., was born in Dorchester County, Md. He was admitted into the Baltimore Conference in 1869, and is now a faithful worker in the Conference. He organized all the work in Kent and Queen Anne's Counties, Md.

HUNTER, CHARLES HENRY, a member of the Virginia Conference, was born in Virginia, June 4, 1843, and was admitted into the Virginia Conference 1872.

HUNTER, GEORGE H., a member of the North Carolina Conference, was born in North Carolina and admitted into the Conference in 1871.

HUNTER, WILLIAM H., was born in Raleigh, N. C., and was taken by his parents to Brooklyn, N. Y., in 1842, where he grew up. After he was licensed to preach he was appointed to fill a vacancy on the Oxford Circuit, Pa., and whilst there attended the Ashman Institute (now Lincoln University). In 1858 he was admitted to the Philadelphia Conference and transferred to the Baltimore Conference, and stationed at Georgetown, D. C., where he remained two years. In 1860 he went to Wilberforce University, Xenia, Ohio, and remained three years. He then returned to the Baltimore Conference in 1863, and was commissioned Chaplain of the First Colored United States Troops, and was sent to the front. On returning from the army he entered the pastorate and filled Israel Church, Washington, D. C., then Wylie street, Pittsburg, and Allegheny City, Pa. In 1872, he was elected General Business Manager of the Publication Department. In 1876, he was transferred to New England Conference and stationed at Boston, where he purchased the Charles Street Church. He is now stationed at New Bedford, Mass.

HUNTER, W. L., a member of the North Carolina Conference, was a member of the General Conference of 1880.

HUNTSVILLE, Ala. The A. M. E. Church has not been in existence here many years, but it is in a prosperous condition.

HUTTON, HENRY, a member of the Baltimore Conference, was for some years an elder in the M. E. Church, but is now a worthy member of the A. M. E. Church.

J

JACKSON, ADAM, a member of the Mississippi Conference, has filled the position of presiding elder and other stations in the Conference very acceptably.

JACKSON, A. N., a member of the Alabama Conference, was educated at Lincoln University, Pa. He has been successful as a pastor.

JACKSON, BERWELL, at the time of his death was a member of the Georgia Conference.

JACKSON, HENRY A., a late member of the Mississippi Conference, was born in Washington, D. C., and reared in the A. M. E. Church. In 1848 he went to Pittsburg, Pa., and there received license to preach. Afterwards he was admitted into the Ohio Conference, where he labored very successfully for several years, and then was transferred South, where he finished his course.

JACKSON, JOHN W., a most excellent local elder of Sullivan Street A. M. E. Church, New York, has been one of the strong supporters of the Church, and no truer man can be found.

JACKSON, J. W. H., a member of the Illinois Conference, was born a slave in Virginia. He crossed the Potomac River when he was a young man and found his way to

Illinois, and was admitted into the Illinois Conference. He was a delegate to the General Conference of 1880.

JACKSON, THOMAS H., D. D., a member of the Ohio Conference, was born in Philadelphia, Pa., and raised in Kentucky. He went to Wilberforce University when he was a small boy. There he was converted, and joined the A. M. E. Church. He pursued a regular course of studies and graduated with honor. He spent several years in the Southern work, and then returned to the Ohio Conference, where he has filled very prominent stations. At present he is the agent for Wilberforce University, Ohio.

JACKSON, THOMAS W., a late member of the New York Conference, after many years of faithful labor died in peace.

JACKSON, WILLIAM, late a member of the Indiana Conference, was born in Annapolis, Md. He went West when he was a young man, seeking a living as a barber. After entering the Church, he married a remarkable Christian lady, who was a great help to him in his studies as well as in his pastoral work. He died at Galesburg, Ill., in 1873.

JACKSONVILLE, Fla. The A. M. E. Church is large; the membership is about six hundred.

JACOBS, CHARLES S., a member of the Illinois Conference, was admitted in 1872.

JEFFERSON, Mo. The A. M. E. Church was organized in this city, May 1861. A new church was built in 1877. Membership about two hundred.

JEFFERSON, PAUL W., and SILAS H., are twins.

Paul is a member of the South Carolina, while Silas is a member of the Columbia Conference, South Carolina. They are both men of some mind, and are so much alike that it is impossible for any one to tell one from the other unless he is well acquainted with them.

JENIFER, JOHN T., D. D., a member of the New England Conference, was born in Baltimore, Md. Like many of his other brethren, he was not born free and had to seek for freedom. He left his native home for the East, and from there went to California and was admitted into the Conference in 1865. He then returned home and entered Wilberforce University and graduated with honors. He then went to the Arkansas Conference and remained several years. He was transferred to the New England Conference in 1881, and stationed at Boston.

JENKINS, JOSHUA W., a very prominent local elder of New York City, was born in Delaware. He has lived for years in that city, and is a man that is very highly respected.

JOHNS, J. A. M., a member of the New Jersey Conference, was born in one of the West India Islands. He received his education there and united with the Moravian Church. On coming to America he joined the A. M. E. Church, and was then admitted into the Virginia Conference, in which he remained three years. He was then transferred to the New Jersey Conference, and is at present stationed at Trenton.

JOHNSON, FRANK, a member of the North Alabama

Conference, was born August 31, 1848, in Alabama, and was admitted into the Conference in 1878, and is now engaged in the good work.

JOHNSON, GEORGE W., late of the Virginia Conference, was born in Louisville, Ky., and admitted into the Indiana Conference in 1838. After spending eight or nine years in said Conference, he came East and received appointments to Philadelphia and New York. He completed his course in Virginia in 1879.

JOHNSON, GEORGE WASHINGTON, a member of the Baltimore Conference, was formerly a member of the British M. E. Church. He was admitted into the Baltimore Conference in 1877.

JOHNSON, HENRY A., a member of the Columbia Conference, South Carolina, was a delegate to the General Conference of 1880.

JOHNSON, HENRY, J., a superannuated member of the New England Conference, was born a slave in Maryland and left there when he was but a boy. On his way through the state of Delaware he was arrested and put in New Castle jail as a runaway slave. When he entered the jail he had the presence of mind to get a fellow prisoner to cut off his hair. In a few days after the advertisement appeared in the papers, and he was represented as a "boy having very full and long hair." The authorities soon became convinced, from his appearance, that he did not answer the description given in the papers, and therefore discharged him. He then made his way on to Philadelphia, and from there to New York, where he joined the A. M. E. Church. He was afterward admitted into the New York Conference, and for many years filled important charges. He is now living in the city of New Bedford, Mass.

JOHNSON, JAMES HENRY ANDREW, D. D., was born in Baltimore City and learned the trade of a barber, and also received a good education. He soon distinguished himself as a debater in the societies. In 1865 he was admitted into the Baltimore Conference, and transferred to South Carolina Conference. But the climate did not agree with him, and so he returned to the Baltimore Conference, and was sent to Princeton, New Jersey, where he attended the Theological Seminary. In 1870 he returned to the Baltimore Conference. In 1872 he was elected Secretary of the General Conference. He is now a presiding elder in the Baltimore Conference.

JOHNSON, LINNEAS, a remarkable layman of Bethel Church, Philadelphia, was born in Baltimore, Md. He led the singing for many years in the church before the choir was introduced, and he also led the choir after it was organized. During his last illness he told his friends when he would die, and when the hour arrived got up from the chair where he was sitting, went to the bed, laid down and in a few moments was gone.

JOHNSON, ROBERT A., a member of the Ohio Conference, was born in Maryland, where he spent his youth. After his conversion he went out as an evangelist with

Thomas Sunrise (the Indian preacher), but on reaching Ohio united with the A. M. E. Church, and was subsequently admitted into the Ohio Conference. Since that time he has filled nearly all the stations of prominence in the Conference. He was a fraternal delegate to the General Conference of the M. E. Church in 1880.

JOHNSON, WILLIAM, a late member of the New England Conference, was born in Easton, Md. At an early age he united with the A. M. E. Church, and being a slave, early started for the land of the free. He settled in Boston, Mass., and served the Church for some years as a local preacher, and was then admitted into the New England Conference. After working faithfully, he died a few years ago.

JOHNSON, WILLIAM D., a member of the Georgia Conference, was born in Baltimore City. He graduated from Lincoln University and went South, where he has labored successfully for some years. He is now stationed at Athens, Ga.

JOHNSON, WILLIAM E., a member of the South Carolina Conference, was born in South Carolina and admitted to the South Carolina Conference in 1867. He has represented his county several times in the State Senate, and is now a presiding elder in the South Carolina Conference.

JOHNSON, W. J., a member of the Ohio Conference, was born in Richmond, Va., Nov. 30, 1846. In 1864, he went into the army, and after retiring from it was admitted into the Conference in 1874. He graduated from Wilberforce University, June 1880, and is stationed at Cambridge, Ohio.

JOHNSON, WILLIAM M., a member of the Baltimore Conference, was born in Western Maryland. He left there for Pennsylvania and spent some years. Afterwards he was received into the New York Conference and transferred to the Baltimore Conference, where he is now laboring.

JOHNSTON, MOSES R., late of the Tennessee Conference, was born in Pennsylvania, graduated from one of the Presbyterian Colleges, and entered the ministry of that Church. He subsequently joined the Tennessee Conference and received appointment to St. John Chapel, Nashville, Tenn. A severe affection of the throat finally terminated in his death. He died in peace.

JOINES, E. C., a member of the Illinois Conference, was born in Illinois. He occupies a high position in the Conference of which he is a member. He was a delegate to the General Conference of 1880.

JONES, ALLEN, one of the oldest members of the Florida Conference, was born a slave in Queen Anne's County, Md., and was sold South long before the war. He was among the first that united with the A. M. E. Church when organized by Rev. Charles H. Pearce.

JONES, ARTHUR, a member of the Baltimore Conference, was born in Maryland. In 1868 he was admitted into the Baltimore Conference and ever since then has been in the active work.

JONES, CHRISTOPHER, SR., a very worthy local

preacher of Cecilton, Md., was among the first who identified himself with the A. M. E. Church in that county. He was a man of standing in the county, and died at a good old age.

JONES, CHRISTOPHER, JR., a member of the Baltimore Conference, was born in Cecil County, Md., Dec. 12, 1846. He was admitted 1880. He is now in Baltimore, Md.

JONES, JOHN P., a layman of Baltimore and a member of Bethel Church, is one of the oldest male members of the Church, having joined in his youth.

JONES, PETER, a worthy layman of the Union Church, Philadelphia, Pa., at the time of his death was the oldest male member of the Church.

JONES, S. B., of the Georgia Conference, is a presiding elder, and was one of the first that entered the Conference when it was organized. He is one of the strong men of the Conference.

JONES, SUGARS P., a member of the Pittsburg Conference, is the oldest minister in the Conference, having been in the regular work for more than thirty years. He has always been respected by the members and ministers.

JONES, WILLIS, was a venerable local deacon of Brooklyn, N. Y. At the time of his death he was the oldest local minister in the Church. He was highly respected by all who knew him.

JONES, W. L., a member of the Florida Conference, at present is the pastor of the Church at Chattahoochee, Fla.

JORDON, ——, one of the oldest female members of Bethel Church, Philadelphia, was always called by younger persons Mother Jordon. She was found ready when the Master called her.

JORDON, ANNETTA, the wife of the Rev. John Jordon, was a great worker for the Church, and no one did more for it in her day. She, like her husband, has gone on to the better land.

JORDON, JOHN, a very worthy layman and class leader in the Church at Norfolk, Va., died a few years ago. His place has been hard to fill.

JORDON, JOHN, a local elder of Baltimore, Md., was present the first Sunday Bethel Church was opened. When he grew up to be a man he joined the A. M. E. Church, and was soon after licensed to preach, and then ordained a deacon by Bishop Morris Brown, and an elder by Bishop Quinn. He died January 1864.

JORDON, JOHN A., a member of the Indiana Conference, was born in one of the Southern states, was admitted into the Indiana Conference in 1873, and has been a faithful worker ever since.

K

KALAMAZOO, Mich., is a flourishing town. The A. M. E. Church has a fine church building in it, which was dedicated in 1876.

KANSAS CITY, Mo., is a city that has sprung up since

the war. The A. M. E. Church has grown as rapidly as the city.

KANSAS CONFERENCE was set off from the Missouri Conference by the General Conference of 1876, and since then has grown very rapidly.

KENNARD, MARY, a member of Bethel Church, Baltimore, Md., as a Christian woman is highly respected by all who know her. She is a great worker for the Church.

KENTUCKY CONFERENCE of the A. M. E. Church was organized in 1865. Since then it has been divided into two Conferences, the Kentucky and the West Kentucky.

KEOKUK, Iowa. The A. M. E. Church was organized there about fifteen years ago, and the membership is about two hundred.

KEY WEST, Fla. There is an A. M. E. church in this town having about two hundred members.

KNIGHT, HENRY A., a member of the Philadelphia Conference, was born in Kentucky, and was educated at Wilberforce University, Ohio. He is stationed at present at Carlisle, Pa.

KNIGHT, RELIEVEUS, a member of the Illinois Conference, was born in Vincennes, Indiana, September 1838. The city where his parents lived had been visited by many desperadoes and the colored people had been subjected to many outrages. But about the time this son was born there was a change in the state of things and relief came. The father named his son Relieveus. He was admitted into the Conference in 1869, and has continued ever since. He is in charge of Cedar Rapids, Iowa.

KNOX, THOMAS E., a member of the Ohio Conference, has been a success in every charge he has held. At present he is stationed at Hamilton, Ohio.

L

LACEY, S. H., is a member of the West Kentucky Conference. After spending some time at Wilberforce University, he was admitted into the Kentucky Conference.

LAFAYETTE, Ind. The A. M. E. Church has had an existence in this city for several years.

LANCASTER, Ohio. The A. M. E. Church was organized in this town many years ago, and since then has been considered one of the strong points in the circuit. It has about one hundred members.

LANCASTER, Pa., is a beautiful city. The A. M. E. Church was first built in this city in 1824. It has since been burnt down, but has been rebuilt, and is one of the finest buildings in that part of the state in the connection. Membership two hundred.

LANE, JOHN FRANCIS, a member of the Baltimore Conference, was in born Annapolis, Md. He joined the M. E. Church when he was a youth, and was licensed there to preach. In 1862 he withdrew from the M. E. Church, and organized the A. M. E. Church in the city of Annapolis. In April 1862 he was admitted to the Baltimore Conference. After filling several stations in that Conference, he was transferred to the Virginia Conference and filled the Portsmouth Station for three years. During his stay in that station he secured the church property to the A. M. E. Connection. He then returned to his old Conference, where he continues to labor very acceptably.

LANKFORD, W. S., a very talented member of the Indiana Conference, was born, raised and educated in his native state. He is one among the finest preachers in the Conference, and is a finished scribe.

LAWRENCE, THOMAS, late of the Ohio Conference, was one of the early western pioneers who assisted with Bishop Quinn in planting the standard of African Methodism west of the mountains. He filled many of the important stations in Western Pennsylvania and Ohio. The last charge he had was Pittsburg, Pa. He retired one night in his usual health, and some time before morning was attacked with the cholera and died in a short time.

LAWS, WILLIAM J., was born in New York City and was educated at Lincoln University, Pa. He was subsequently admitted into the New York Conference. He was then transferred to the New England Conference, and has filled some of the largest charges in the Conference. He was elected to represent his Conference in the General Conference of 1880.

LAY DELEGATES were first admitted into the General Conference of the A. M. E. Church, in 1872, at Nashville, Tenn. They are elected by an electoral college called for that purpose, and confirmed by the Annual Conferences previous to the General Conference.

LEAVENWORTH, Kansas. The A. M. E. church of this city is one of the oldest in the state. It was built in 1862, and is one of the largest stations in the Kansas Conference. The membership is about four hundred.

LEE, BENJAMIN FRANKLIN, President of the Wilberforce University, Ohio, was born in Salem, New Jersey, where he lived until he was a man grown, and then went to Wilberforce to take care of the horses. He then commenced a course of studies and graduated with honors, and became for a time one of the professors, and since has been elected the President of the University of which he was once the hostler.

LEE, BENJAMIN HENRY, a member of the Baltimore Conference, was born a slave in Winchester, Va. During the war he left and found his way to Ohio, where he joined the A. M. E. Church. Subsequently he was admitted into the Ohio Conference, and then transferred to the Baltimore Conference, in which he is laboring successfully.

LEE, HENRIETTA, the widow of Rev. Levin Lee, was born and raised in Baltimore, Md. She is one of the oldest female members of Bethel Church, Baltimore. Her first husband was Rev. Thomas Williams, a local deacon. She was married to her last husband, Rev. Levin Lee, in 1854.

LEE, JOHN, a local preacher of Georgetown, D. C., was one of the first members and class leaders of the A. M. E. Church of that city. He lived and died a faithful Christian man.

LEE, JOSEPH H., a layman of Baltimore, is a son of the late Rev. Levin Lee. He has served the Church as a class leader and steward.

LEE, LEVIN, a late member of the Baltimore Conference, was born in Baltimore, Md. He was raised in the family of Dr. Burket, who taught him to read and write. In his youth he joined the A. M. E. Church, was licensed in 1824, and was admitted into the Baltimore Conference in 1842. He was secretary of the Conference for many years, and also filled important stations in the Conference. In October, 1858, he closed his earthly career and was buried from Bethel Church, Baltimore, Md.

LEE, WATKINS, formerly a member of the Ohio Conference, was an earnest and plain preacher. He spent nearly twenty years in the service of the Church, and passed away to be forever with the Lord.

LEE, XENOPHON, a very worthy local deacon of Brownsville, Pa., was born a slave in Virginia, but went to Pennsylvania and there accumulated property, and lived and died respected by all who knew him.

LEWIS, ABRAM D., an eminent local minister of Pittsburg, Pa., was for some years the secretary of the Conference. At the General Conference of 1840, he was the great advocate of the course of studies that were proposed for candidates entering the ministry. He succeeded in having the matter passed.

LEWIS, HARRISON H., at present a member of the New York Conference, was born in Caroline County, Md., and raised in the State of Delaware. In 1865 he was admitted into the Philadelphia Conference, and continued therein until he was transferred to the New York Conference, where he distinguished himself as an able preacher.

LEWIS, JEREMIAH, an aged member of the Ohio Conference, was born in North Carolina and went to Ohio when he was a young man. There he united with the A. M. E. Church, and was afterward admitted into the Conference. For years he has been regarded as a strong man.

LEWIS, JOHN W., a young member of the Ohio Conference, joined the A. M. E. Church at Delaware, Ohio, and from there he was recommended to the Conference and was received.

LEWIS, MORRIS, a member of the Indiana Conference, was born a slave in the state of Missouri. After he grew up to be a man he got it into his head to cross over the Mississippi River to Illinois and go as far as Chicago, where he joined the A. M. E. Church. He soon showed signs of future usefulness. Subsequently he was admitted into the Indiana Conference, where he has labored ever since with great acceptability.

LEWIS, PETER, for many years a member of the Philadelphia Conference, was born and raised in the State of Delaware, and ordained by Bishop Allen. His labors were confined to his native state, in which he organized many churches. A few years ago he went to Canada, and there died at a good old age.

LEWIS, S. LEWIS, late of the Indiana Conference, for many years was a member of the New York and New England Conferences. In 1872 he was transferred to the Indiana Conference, and stationed at Vincennes. He entered upon his work cheerfully and very soon the Church commenced to look up; but they were destined to be disappointed, for his career was short. He soon sickened and died in peace.

LEXINGTON, Ky., is a fine city. The A. M. E. Church was organized here by Rev. David Smith in 1865. The first pastor appointed was Rev. G. H. Graham, of Ohio. The first Annual Conference was held there in 1867. The church has been greatly improved since, and is now a very fine edifice.

LEXINGTON, Mo., is situated on the Missouri River. The A. M. E. Church was organized in this city in 1867. They worshipped for some time in a small frame church; since then a large brick church has been erected.

LINDSAY, I. N., a young member of the Kentucky Conference, was born in one of the Southern states. He was a soldier in the late war. After leaving the army he went to Delaware, Ohio, and there united with the A. M. E. Church. He was afterwards admitted into the Ohio Conference and transferred to the Kentucky Conference. He has continued to do good work in that Conference as a presiding elder as well as a stationed pastor.

LITTLE ROCK, Arkansas. The A. M. E. Church was organized in this city soon after the close of the late war, and it is now one of the finest charges in that Conference.

LLOYD, BENJAMIN, F., a member of the Virginia Conference, was born in Wilmington, Del., April 25, 1844. When he reached manhood he went to sea and was shipwrecked, but was picked up by a ship and taken to Liverpool. On his return home he was admitted into the Conference. He studied at Howard University, Washington, D. C. He is now a member of the Virginia Conference.

LOCAL PREACHER. This class of ministers have been recognized in the A. M. E. Church from the day of its organization to the present. For many years they outnumbered the traveling preachers in the Annual Conferences, for they were admitted to membership and were entitled to the same rights and privileges as the traveling preachers had.

LOCKS, JOHN W., a highly respected layman in Bethel Church, Baltimore, Md., has been a leader and trustee for more than twenty-five years, and is one of the best business men in the city; and was among the first colored men that served on the grand jury of the United States Court in Baltimore, Md.

LOGANSPORT, Ind., is among the oldest charges in that part of the state. The church is new and the congregation and membership large.

LONG, M. R. J., a member of the Philadelphia Conference, was born in Princeton, N. J., Feb. 18, 1847, admitted into the New Jersey Conference 1872, and is a man of some importance.

LOUISIANA CONFERENCE of the A. M. E. Church was organized soon after the close of the late war.

LOUISVILLE, Ky., is a large city. The A. M. E. Church was organized in this city many years ago by Bishop Quinn. The first church that was built there was called Quinn Chapel. A few years afterward the Asbury Chapel, on Ninth street, united with the A. M. E. Church. There are now Quinn, Asbury, St. James and Young's Chapels. They all have separate pastors.

LYNCH, BENJAMIN, a late member of the Philadelphia Conference, was born in Baltimore, Md. After he was licensed to preach in the A. M. E. Church, he withdrew and united with the Presbyterians and remained there some time, and then returned home again and filled very acceptably stations in New Jersey and New York. He was then transferred to the Philadelphia Conference and finished his course at Milford, Delaware.

LYNCH, JAMES, a son of Rev. Benjamin Lynch, was born in Baltimore, Md. When a little boy he was a pupil of Bishop Payne's, and afterwards went to a college in the East. In 1859 he was admitted into the Indiana Conference. In 1860 he was transferred to the Baltimore Conference, where he remained for a few years and then went to South Carolina as a missionary. He succeeded in organizing churches in several parts of the State, and went to Georgia and organized churches there. In 1865 he was appointed by the Bishop editor of the "Christian Recorder." He resigned in 1866, and joined the M. E.

Church, and went to Jackson, Miss. After filling many stations and districts, he was elected Secretary of the State. He was a very eloquent speaker, but died in the prime of life.

MACABE, SOLOMON, is a well-to-do layman of Bethel Church, Baltimore, Md. He was born in Elkton, Md., and went to Baltimore when he was a young man. He learned the barber's trade, and accumulated considerable wealth. He is a strong friend of the Church, and always ready to help when called upon.

MACGHEE, A. J., a member of the North Georgia Conference, was a delegate to the General Conference of 1880.

MACINTOSH, ANEAS, a late member of the Indiana Conference, was born in Vincennes, Ind., taken into the Church by Bishop Quinn, admitted into the Conference when a young man and educated at one of the high schools of Indiana. He for many years was the leading man in the Conference, and one of the finest writers of his day. His last appointment was Bloomington, Ill. He went to it full of enthusiasm, but in the winter of 1865 his health failed him. It soon became apparent that his work was done, and that he would die. He sent for his wife and children to come from the city of Chicago to Bloomington to see him die. When his wife came he said to her, "Fannie, this is the last of your husband Mac. Fannie, I die all right." This was the last he said. He then passed away.

MACON CITY, Mo. The A. M. E. Church was organized in this city by Rev. Thomas W. Henderson. The first church was built in 1867. It was a small frame building. In 1876 a large brick church was erected. Membership three hundred.

MACON, Ga., is a large city. Here the Georgia Conference was organized in 1867. The A. M. E. Church is a large, commodious brick building, and the society is formed of seven hundred persons.

MADISON, Fla. The A. M. E. Church was organized here soon after the war, and has been one of the leading appointments in the Conference.

MADISON, Ind. The A. M. E. Church has had an existence here for some years, but has not been able to do much. The membership is rather small.

MADISON, JAMES, a member of the Missouri Conference, is one of her ablest sons. He was among the first sent out into certain parts of the State as missionaries. He succeeded admirably.

MADISON, JAMES H., late of the Louisiana Conference, was born in Missouri a slave. Soon after the late war he went to New England and entered school. He was then admitted into the New England Conference, and very soon became one of its leaders. He was a delegate to the General Conference of 1876, and was afterward transferred to the Louisiana Conference and appointed to New Orleans, La. He entered upon his work with a grand prospect before him; but, alas! his career was short. The yellow fever broke out in the city and his members died very fast, but he would not leave them. He was found among the sick and dying, doing what he could for them, believing, as he said, it was his duty to stay with them. He was finally attacked with the disease, and in a few days was no more. He died at his post.

MADISON, N. J., is a flourishing town. The A. M. E. Church has existed here for some years.

MALONE, JOHN WILLIAM, a member of the Illinois Conference, was born in North Carolina, Jan. 22, 1831, and went to Indiana, 1837; joined the A. M. E. Church 1854; admitted into the Indiana Conference 1865, and has since filled the most of the important charges in his Conference.

MARIETTA, Ohio. There is a small A. M. E. Church in this town. The membership has for many years been small.

MARIETTA, Pa., is an old town situated on the Pennsylvania railroad. The A. M. E. Church is one of the oldest appointments in that part of the State.

MARTIN, JOHN, a worthy local deacon of Port Deposit, Md., was born and raised in Cecil County. He was a great friend to the Church. He raised a large family of children, who, also, like their father, love the Church He died in 1864.

MAYVILLE, Cal., is a small town. The A. M. E. Church was planted in this town by one of the missionaries who went to California early. The church there is small and also the membership.

MASON, DANIEL N., a member of the Ohio Conference, was born in Kent County, Delaware. His father, Thomas Mason, was one of the founders of African Methodism in that part of Delaware. Daniel learned the carpenter trade, and then went to New England. He was there admitted into the Conference. In 1876 he was transferred to the Ohio Conference, where he has labored very successfully.

MASSEY, ANDREW, a late member of the Philadelphia Conference, was born and raised in the State of Delaware and was one of the early pioneers of African Methodism in that State. He organized a great many churches, and died at the age of nearly one hundred.

MAXWELL, GEORGE, a young member of the Ohio Conference, was born in Xenia, Ohio, and there educated. He was admitted into the Ohio Conference in 1875.

MAXWELL, WILLIAM T., a member of the Ohio Conference, was born in Pennsylvania, and was admitted into the Philadelphia Conference. In 1877 he was transferred to the Ohio Conference and stationed at Walnut Hills. Whilst there he entered one of the colleges, and sustained himself very creditably. He is stationed at present at Dayton, Ohio.

MEACHEM, ROBERT, a Presiding Elder of the Florida Conference, was one of the first A. M. E. Church preachers in that State. Soon after that there was an organization in Charleston S. C. Robert Meachem then went from Tallahassee, Florida, to Charleston, was received by Rev. R. H. Cain, licensed and sent back home to raise the A. M. E.

Church flag, and he succeeded. In addition to his ministerial work he has been a State Senator for many years.

MEMPHIS, Tenn., is situated on the Mississippi River, and is said to be the largest city between St. Louis and New Orleans. African Methodism was introduced into this city by the late Rev. Austin Woodfork. There are now five Churches in the city—Avery Chapel, St. Andrew, St. James, Providence and Mount Zion. They are all in good condition.

MERRY, LOUIS N., one of the fathers of the Tennessee Conference, was born and raised in the city of Nashville, Tenn. He was among the first preachers that united with the A. M. E. Church when it was first organized, and has filled the most prominent charges in the Conference. He is a very popular preacher, and is highly respected as a pastor wherever he is known.

MIDDLETON, WILLIAM H., a layman of Bordentown, New Jersey, for many years was the leading man in the Church, and was steward and trustee. He was an employe of the railroad company, and met with an accident that resulted in his death. His place has been hard to fill.

MIDDLETOWN, New York, has a small A. M. E. Church, a membership of about ninety, and a good Sunday school.

MIDDLETOWN, Ohio, is on the Cincinnati, Hamilton and Dayton Railroad. The A. M. E. Church is small—a membership of about thirty.

MILES, RICHARD, a young member of the Baltimore Conference, was born in one of the Southern States. He went to Annapolis, Md., and spent a few years. In 1877 he was admitted into the Baltimore Conference. He is now filling a station in Baltimore City.

MILLER, JEREMIAH, one of the pioneers of the Church —a very large man—was born in some part of Maryland. He entered the Conference in those days when it cost something to be an itinerant preacher. He was arrested once and put in the jail at Easton, Md., but told the authorities that if he was not released, the Lord would send a judgment on the town. The County Court was then in session, and there arose a great storm, which so alarmed the citizens that the judge ordered the sheriff to go and let that old preacher out or they would be destroyed. His orders were obeyed, and Miller came out and mounted his horse and left the town, and returned no more.

MILLER, JEREMIAH, a nephew of Rev. Jeremiah Miller, was born a slave in Kent county, Md. He left there when he was a young man for Pennsylvania, where he got some one to assist him in purchasing his freedom. After he obtained the freedom of his body he thought it was time for him to seek for the freedom of his soul. He then obtained it and was licensed as a local preacher, and settled in the town of West Chester, Pa., where he spent his days. On returning from church one Sunday he was taken ill, and lying down upon the bed said to his friends "My work is done." He then fell asleep.

MITCHEL, L. M., a member of the North Mississippi Conference, was a delegate to the General Conference of 1880.

MITCHELL, JOHN G., D. D., a member of the Ohio Conference was educated at Oberlin College, Ohio. He was for some time professor in Wilberforce University, Ohio. After leaving that institution he went South, and was there admitted into the Conference. Since then, he has filled Asbury Chapel, Louisville, Ky., and then Wylie Avenue, Pittsburg, Pa., and at present is stationed at Zanesville, Ohio. Dr. Mitchell is one of the finest scholars in the Church.

MITCHELL, MARIA, was a very aged female member of the Ebenezer Church, in Baltimore. She was called by all who knew her—Mother Mitchell. She used to walk out in the aisle of the church at Lovefeast to view the army. She was ready when the summons came for her.

MITCHELL, NATHAN, of the Ohio Conference, was admitted in 1876, and has moved steadily onward until he ranks among the useful young ministers of the Conference.

MITCHELL, WILLIAM DAVID, a member of the Ohio Conference, was born in North Carolina. He left that State for Ohio when he was quite young, and settled on a farm. Afterwards he was admitted into the Ohio Conference, where he has labored with great success to the present. He is a great revivalist, for wherever he is appointed the Church is revived.

MITCHEM, JOHNSTON, a member of the Indiana Conference, was born in Kentucky, and removed into Indiana when he was a young man. He united with the A. M. E. Church, and was admitted into the Conference. He has been recognized as one of her very worthy sons.

MITCHEM, NATHAN, was born in Kentucky. On moving to Indiana, he engaged in farming for some time. Afterward he entered the Indiana Conference, and after filling some of the most important charges, was transferred to the Tennessee Conference and stationed at Nashville. While there he built the grand St. Paul Chapel, which was considered one of the finest church buildings in the state, belonging to the A. M. E. Church. He has the name of being the great church builder of the A. M. E. Church.

MOORE, DANIEL WILKINS, was born in Kent county, Md., in 1802. He went to Baltimore city when he was a young man, and, after his conversion, joined the A. M. E. Church. For years he taught a day school in Ebenezer Church, Baltimore. After having been ordained a local deacon he felt it his duty to enter into the work more fully, and so was appointed by the Bishop to supply Port Deposit Circuit. The next year he was admitted into the Conference, and soon began to take his place by the side of the ablest men in the Conference. He was considered one of the best theologians of the Conference in his day. He filled the most important stations in the Conference. His constitution finally gave way, and he asked and obtained a superannuated relation, which he sustained for several years. In the autumn of 1877 he was taken sick. It was evident that his earthly career was near its end. He said to a brother who went to see him :."I am going to die," and "I am no more afraid of dying then I am of going out at that door, for every thing is right between me and my Maker ; and if there is any thing wrong I don't know it." In a few weeks thereafter he went to sleep in death.

MOORE, JACOB E. WATERS, a member of the Virginia Conference, was born in Baltimore, Md., January 26, 1847, and was admitted into the Virginia Conference in 1869. He has continued in active service ever since. He has been one of the secretaries of the Conference for some years, and was a delegate to the General Conference of 1880.

MOORE, JACOB MARTIN, was born in Kent county, Md. He was licensed in the M. E. Church, but resigned in 1840 and organized an independent church. In 1847 he and his church united with the Baltimore Conference of the A. M. E. Church and remained in it until 1850. He then left the United States for Liberia, Africa, and there united with the M. E. Church. After spending several years in that country, filling prominent positions both in Church and State, he died.

MOORE, M. M., a member of the North Carolina Conference, occupies a high position in the Conference.

MOORE, WILLIAM, late member of the Philadelphia Conference was born in Cecil county, Md., and was converted at the residence of General Sewell, about a mile Southeast of the town of Elkton. After he felt it to be his duty to preach he united with the Philadelphia Conference. Having no early educational advantages he was kept back for years, but he finally came to the front, and for more than thirty years was among the leading men. He was a very hard student and a very able preacher. He filled nearly all the prominent stations in the Baltimore, Philadelphia and New York Conferences. He sustained a Superannuated relation to the Conference for several years, and lived in the city of Philadelphia. In 1871 he was getting ready to visit the New York Conference to see his old friends (for he had many there), when his Master called for him and found him ready. He died very suddenly and was buried from Bethel Church, Philadelphia.

MOORE, WILLIAM, a member of the Florida Conference, is at present stationed at Mariana, and is regarded as a strong man.

MORGAN, JOHN R. V., late of the California Conference, was born in Kent county, Md., and was raised in the city of Philadelphia. When he was a boy there was an aptness in him that was admired by all who knew him. He was very wild, but when he embraced religion he gave evidence of future usefulness. In 1847 he was sent by the Bishop to Salem Circuit, N. J., as an assistant to the minister in charge. He soon attracted the attention of the people. In 1848 he was admitted into the Philadelphia Conference. When the late war broke out he went into the army, and there he distinguished himself for bravery. On returning from the army he commenced working again, and went into the New England Conference. From there he was transferred to the California Conference and stationed at San Francisco, where he spent two or three years. From there he went to Denver City, Colorado, and after spending a month or two there, was summoned away by death. It is said by one who stood by him when dying, that he said: "This is the last of John R. V. Morgan."

MORGAN, JOSEPH H., a member of the New Jersey Conference, was born in Philadelphia, Pa., 1843, and was admitted into the Philadelphia Conference 1876. He was transferred to the New York Conference, and remained there until 1880, when he was transferred to the New Jersey Conference, where he is now laboring. He was a delegate to the General Conference of 1880.

MORGAN, WILLIAM, a late member of the Ohio Conference, was born in Kentucky. He was licensed in the M. E. Church. On coming into the State of Ohio, he united with the A. M. E. Church and Conference, and for more than twenty-five years was regarded as one of the strongest preachers in the Conference. He was very much respected wherever known. When old age came on he asked and obtained a superannuated relation, in which he continued until the end of his days.

MORRIS, B. W., a member of the North Carolina Conference, was born in Newbern, N. C. After he grew up to be a man he went East, and there he educated himself and then returned to his native State, and for several years represented his county in the State Legislature. In 1868 he was admitted into the North Carolina Conference, and since then has filled stations of prominence in the Conference.

MORRIS, JAMES M., a young, talented and eloquent minister, son of Jarrett Morris, was born in Providence, R. I., and was educated at Lincoln University, Pa. After he graduated he went to Boston, Mass., and entered the Theological School, and came out in brilliant colors. He then went to South Carolina and spent several years, but the climate did not agree with him. He returned home, and was soon called away to the better land.

MORRIS, JAMES T., a member of the Baltimore Conference, was born in King and Queen county, Va., March 4, 1840, and admitted into the Virginia Conference 1870. He spent two or three years in Virginia, and was then transferred to the Baltimore Conference, where he is now at work. He spent some time at Howard University, Washington, D. C.

MORRIS, JARRETT, was a worthy layman of Providence, R. I. He was elected a lay delegate to the General Conference of 1876. Since then he has gone the way of all the earth, leaving an interesting Christian family behind.

MORRIS, JEREMIAH M., a member of the Pittsburg Conference, was born in Ohio, and educated at a College in Springfield, Ohio. He is a profound thinker and an excellent pastor. He is at present stationed at the Wylie Avenue Church, Pittsburg, Pa.

MORRISTOWN, N. J., is a beautiful little town. The A. M. E. Church was organized in this town in 1842 by the late Rev. H. C. Turner. Since then many changes have taken place, but she still maintains an existence and a stationed pastor.

MORSELL, CHARLES W., the very efficient missionary to Hayti, is the son of a worthy layman, formerly of Baltimore, but now of Lockport, N. Y. He graduated from Lincoln University, Pa., and entered the South Carolina Conference, where he did a grand work. He was called by the Bishops to leave the South and cross the ocean to Hayti to take charge of that interesting mission. He obeyed, and soon, with his youthful wife, sailed from New York. He reached the island in safety, and went to work. Great success has attended his efforts.

MORTON, W. D., a member and presiding elder of the North Alabama Conference, has been an active member of the Conference for some years. He was also a delegate to the General Conference of 1880.

MOUNT PLEASANT, Iowa, is a beautiful town. The African M. E. Church has existed in this place for some years. It has good Church property and a membership of one hundred and fifty, and a flourishing Sunday school.

MOUNT VERNON, Ohio, is the capital of Knox county. The A. M. E. Church has existed in this town for years, but never succeeded until Rev. Daniel N. Mason was appointed there. He went to work and completed the Church, and it was dedicated in the winter of 1877. It is now a station.

MURPHY, BENJAMIN, is one of the oldest choristers of Baltimore. He led the choir of Bethel Church for more then twenty-five years, and at present is the leader of the choir of St. John's A. M. E. Church, in Baltimore, Md.

MURPHY, WILLIAM, an excellent local deacon of Chester, Pa., was born in Baltimore, Md., where he was converted and joined the A. M. E. Church. For years he was one of the leading laymen. He moved from Baltimore to Chester, Pa., where he has lived for a number of years, and is very much respected by all classes of the citizens.

MURRAY, ALEXANDER, an aged member of Bethel Church, Baltimore, Md., died long since.

MURRAY, GEORGE, one of the best of men, was born in Queen Anne's county, Md. He has been an exhorter and leader in Bethel Church, Baltimore, for fifty years. He is said to be over a hundred years of age, and goes round to see his members, and is always in his seat in church.

MURRAY, NATHANIEL, a local preacher of Springtown, N. J., was born a slave in Maryland, and when a young man left for New Jersey. He was one of the strong supporters of the Church in that part of New Jersey for years. He died at a good old age.

MURRAY, REUBEN, a local deacon of New York, was born a slave in Caroline county, Md. In 1840 he and his brother left for another part of the country and reached there safely. After he was gone several years, he got a friend of his boyhood to purchase his freedom. In 1868, he was a local delegate to the General Conference, which sat in Washington, D. C. On leaving the Conference he crossed over the Chesapeake bay, and called upon his former master, who failed to recognize him. After visiting a few of his friends he returned to New York, and in a short time passed away.

MURRAY, SAMUEL, a local deacon of Reading, Pa.,

was born in Baltimore, Md., and went to Pennsylvania when he was quite a young man and settled in Reading, Pa. He was instrumental in raising the A. M. E. Church in that town. He was ordained as a deacon in May 1841. He raised a large family of children—one is a very able preacher. The children are all very talented. The old soldier died a few years since at the place then called Attleborough, Pa. His wife Sarah survived him a few years. She died in St. Louis, Mo., in 1881, and was brought home to rest by the side of her husband.

MURRAY, SIMON, a venerable minister of Philadelphia, was born in Caroline County, Md., and died in Philadelphia, 1840.

MUSCATINE, Iowa. The A. M. E. Church has existed in this town for years, and has a membership of about one hundred. Alexander Clark, a layman, has been a great support to the Church, and he was also a lay delegate to the Ecumenical Conference which met in London, September, 1881.

MYER, JOHN, a layman of Baltimore, Md., has been an acceptable member of Bethel Church for many years, and is regarded as an upright Christian man.

MYERS, ISAAC, the Superintendent of the Sunday school of Bethel Church, Baltimore, Md., was born January 23, 1836. He was employed in the United States postal service for ten years. He now is a trustee of the church and secretary of the board.

N

NASHVILLE, Tenn., is the capital of the State. The A. M. E. Church was organized in this city during the late war by Bishop Payne. Since then it has steadily increased. There are six churches now in the city,—St. Paul, St. John, Bethel, Salem, Ebenezer and Payne Chapel.

NELSON, COOK P., a member of the South Carolina Conference, was born Nov. 2, 1851, was admitted into the Conference 1872, and has been engaged actively in the work ever since.

NELSON, JOSEPH H., late a member of the Ohio Conference, was born in Winchester, Va. There he joined the M. E. Church. In 1861 he went to Baltimore, Md., to live, and there joined the A. M. E. Church. In 1864 he was admitted into the Baltimore Conference and thence was transferred to the Philadelphia Conference. For a while he attended Lincoln University. Leaving there he went west and was received by transfer into the Ohio Conference. He filled several stations, and finally ended his pilgrimage in Cleveland, Ohio. He was a very eloquent speaker.

NEW ALBANY, Ind. There is one A. M. E. Church in this city. It was dedicated September, 1872.

NEWARK, N. J. The A. M. E. Church was organized in this city in 1842, and a new church was dedicated in 1868.

NEWARK, Ohio. The A. M. E. Church in this city is small, but the members are hard workers.

NEW BEDFORD, Mass., is a beautiful city. The A. M. E. Church is strong here, and has a fine congregation. The new church was dedicated in 1866.

NEWBERN, N. C., is a large town. The A. M. E. Church was organized in this town soon after the war, by Rev. George A. Rue, who was a native of that town. He had been away for some years, and then returned home and raised the standard there.

NEW BRIGHTON, Pa. The A. M. E. Church is in a fine condition. A new church was dedicated here in 1878.

NEW BRUNSWICK, N. J. African Methodism was planted in this city more than fifty years ago. A new church was built and dedicated here a few years since.

NEW ENGLAND CONFERENCE was organized in 1848. It includes all the New England states.

NEW JERSEY CONFERENCE was organized in 1872, and includes all the state of New Jersey.

NEWMAN, ALFRED, late of the Texas Conference, was born in Winchester, Va., and left when General Banks retreated from there. In 1866, he was admitted into the Ohio Conference. After spending several years in that Conference, he asked for a transfer to Texas. He went there, and soon died.

NEWMAN, WILLIAM, a late member of the Ohio Conference, spent more than thirty years in the itinerant work, traveling circuits and filling stations. He died in middle age.

NEW ORLEANS. This city, it is said, was settled by

the French. It has three A. M. E. Churches,—St. James Chapel, Union Bethel and St. John's.

NEWPORT, R. I. The A. M. E. Church is large in this city, and has a membership of two hundred.

NEWSOME, MATTHEW T., formerly a member of the Ohio Conference, but now a member of one of the Southwestern Conferences, is a minister of some ability and has been in the work for years.

NEWTON, ALEXANDER H., a member of the New Jersey Conference, has labored in Tennessee, Louisiana and North Carolina with great acceptability.

NEW YORK CONFERENCE was organized in 1817 or 1818, and includes the whole state. The church in New York city was for many years located on Second street, but as the people began to move up to the other part of the city, it became necessary to move the church, and therefore the pastor and trustees bought a church on Sullivan Street from the M. E. Church, and it is the most flourishing congregation of color in the city.

NICHLAS, JOSEPH, a member of the Baltimore Conference, was born in the state of Michigan. He first entered the ministry of the A. M. E. Church and then was transferred to the North Carolina Conference, where he remained several years. He was then transferred to the Baltimore Conference, where he is laboring successfully.

NICHOLS, JOHN WESLEY, a layman of Baltimore, Md., was born in Easton, Md. He has lived for many years in Baltimore, and filled the position of steward in the Church.

NICHOLSON, JACOB, a member of the Baltimore Conference, was born in Chestertown, Md. He went to Baltimore when he was a boy and joined the M. E. Church, in which he was licensed and ordained. In 1862, he was admitted into the Baltimore Conference and filled important stations in the Conference. He is regarded as a minister of high moral sense.

NOBLE, WILLIAM H., a member of the Arkansas Conference, was born in Georgia and was admitted into the Conference among the first after its organization. He served both as pastor and presiding elder.

NORFOLK, Va., is a large city. The A. M. E. Church was organized in this city 1863. The church is a large brick building, situated on Bute Street, and is entirely free from debts. This result is attributable to the herculean efforts of the present pastor, Dr. Watkins.

NORRIS, THOMAS, a very worthy layman of Pittsburg Pa., was for many years one of the leading men in the Church. He served the Church as a trustee and steward, and has left a name behind him that will live in the memory of the Church for years.

NORRISTOWN, Pa., is one of the most beautiful little towns in that part of Pennsylvania. The A. M. E. Church has existed in this town for many years. The church building is a good one and the membership is about one hundred.

NORRIS, WILLIAM R., a member of the Philadelphia Conference, was born in Maryland, and served his time with

Bishop Newcomer, of the United Brethren Church. On leaving Maryland he settled in Salem, New Jersey, where, as a local preacher, he was very acceptable. He was admitted into the Philadelphia Conference in 1863, and no minister of the Conference has done better work than he.

NORTH ALABAMA CONFERENCE, is part of the original Alabama Conference. The growth was so very rapid within the last few years that it was thought best to divide it. Bishop Campbell, then Presiding Bishop, agreed to it and the object was effected.

NORTH CAROLINA CONFERENCE was organized at Greensboro', N. C., by Bishop Wayman and it includes the entire state.

NORTH GEORGIA CONFERENCE is a part of the original Georgia Conference. The Georgia and North Georgia Conferences are two of the largest Conferences in the Connection.

O

OFFER, JOHN H., a member of the Virginia Conference, was born in Annapolis, Md. There he joined the M. E. Church. On moving to Baltimore City he united with the A. M. E. Church. In 1863 he went into the army, and after his discharge entered the Baltimore Conference. He was subsequently transferred to the Virginia Conference where he has labored with success ever since.

OFFER, WILLIAM H., of the Kansas Conference, was

born in Annapolis, Md. He moved to Philadelphia when a young man and joined the A. M. E. Church. In 1862 he was admitted into the Philadelphia Conference, and in 1865 was transferred to the California Conference, where he remained until 1880, when he was transferred to the Kansas Conference, where he is now laboring.

OGLETON, WILLIAM H., a member of the Tennessee Conference, was born in Washington County, Md., March 1, 1842, and admitted into the Tennessee Conference 1873. He was educated at the Central Tennessee College, Nashville, and is now stationed at Fayetteville, Tenn.

OHIO CONFERENCE, fourth in age, includes all the State of Ohio, except Salem, Youngstown and Warren, which are in the Pittsburg Conference.

OLGEE, GILBERT, is a member of the West Tennessee Conference. He has served several years as presiding elder, and is now filling an important charge.

ONLY, PHILIP M., a member of the Virginia Conference, was born in Maryland, and was admitted into the Baltimore Conference in 1879, and was transferred to the Virginia Conference, where he has worked ever since.

OMAHA, Neb. The A. M. E. Church has been in this city for some years, and has a good church property and membership.

ORANGE, N. J., is a beautiful little town. The A. M. E. Church was organized there about twenty years since. The corner stone for the first building was laid in 1866, and the dedication took place in October, 1866.

OSKALOOSA, Iowa. The A. M. E. Church was organized in 1872. Membership one hundred and a good Sunday School.

OTTAWA, Ill. The A. M. E. Church has seventy-five members, good church property and a flourishing Sunday School.

OUSLEY, WILLIAM B., is one of the oldest members of the Missouri Conference. He was among the first that went into the interior of the State and did a grand work.

OWEGO, N. Y. This town is situated on several rail roads. The A. M. E. Church is the only colored Methodist Church in the town, and is in an excellent condition.

OWEN, JAMES C., a member of the Missouri Conference, was born and raised in Hannibal, Mo. In 1872 he was admitted into the Missouri Conference. He has gradually come to the front, and is now considered one of the strong men of the Conference. He was a member of the General Conference of 1880.

OWEN, JAMES, a very worthy local deacon of Baltimore county, for years has been engaged in farming, and is regarded as a citizen of great Christian integrity.

OWEN, DAVID, an esteemed local deacon of the Church at Portsmouth, Va., was a great help to the pastor. He died a few years ago.

OWENSBORO, Ky., is situated on the Ohio River. The A. M. E. Church is reported to have about one hundred and fifteen members and a fine Sunday School here.

P

PADUCAH, Ky., is situated on the Ohio River. The A. M. E. Church has a very large congregation and membership here. The church was finished and dedicated in 1876.

PALAMER, JAMES, a layman of Newport, R. I., was born in Maryland and lived in Baltimore for years, but he is now settled in Newport, R. I., and takes a prominent part in the affairs of the Church.

PALMER, JOHN M., and HERBERT, members of the Pittsburg Conference, were born in Lewistown, Pa., and admitted into the Conference in 1878. They are small in stature, but are destined to be large in intellect.

PARKER, RICHARD H., a late member of the Virginia Conference, was born a slave in Norfolk, Va., and remained until the emancipation. He was then advanced in life. He was among the eight hundred that united with the A. M. E. Church in Norfolk, Va., in 1863. He was admitted into the Conference in 1864, and, although rather advanced in life, he did a grand work. He died a few years ago and the children of the Sunday School erected a monument of marble to his memory.

PARKER, BYARD, of the Indiana Conference, was born a slave in Missouri and was a man of eloquence. He went to Iowa and there died.

PATTERSON, LEONARD, at present a member of the Philadelphia Conference, was born and raised in New York

State. He had the advantage of a good common school education, and for several years was employed by the School Board of the town where he lived as a teacher. In this position he succeeded admirably. Afterward he was admitted into the New York Conference, and for years acted as the Secretary of that Conference. He is one of the best short-hand writers in the Church. He is now stationed at Frankford, Pa.

PATTERSON, MADISON, a late venerable member of the Indiana Conference, was born in North Carolina and spent most of his days in his adopted State. At the time of his death he was the oldest member of the Indiana Conference.

PEARCE, CHARLES H., a member of the East Florida Conference, was born a slave in Queen Anne's County, Md. He purchased his freedom and was licensed in the M. E. Church. In 1852 he was admitted into the New England Conference, where he spent a short time. He then went to Canada and remained there until after the war. Then he returned to the United States, went to Florida and organized the A. M. E. Church. He was a State Senator for several years, and now fills the largest station in the Conference, viz., Jacksonville, Florida.

PEARCE, THOMAS T., late a member of the Philadelphia Conference, went to Hayti some years ago to see what he could do in raising the standard of African Methodism there, but he didn't succeed, and so returned home to the United States, and died a member of the Philadelphia Conference.

PEARCE, JAMES V., a member of the New Jersey Conference, was born in Gouldtown, N. J. He joined the Church in 1846, and subsequently was admitted into the Conference. He has been a good worker ever since.

PEARCE, JEHU H., a young member of the New Jersey Conference, was born in New Jersey, and admitted into the New Jersey Conference in 1878. He is now filling Allentown appointment.

PECK, NATHANIEL, a local elder of Baltimore, was born in Baltimore, Md. At an early age he entered the A. M. E. Church. In 1840 he was sent by the colored people of Baltimore to the island of Trinidad. He was accompanied by another minister who was a member of the M. E. Church. Their report was read with interest by the colored people of the State. Mr. Peck raised a large family of children. Two of his sons are in the ministry—Francis J., is in the A. M. E. Church, and Edward W. S., in the M. E. Church. In 1848 Mr. Peck withdrew from the A. M. E. Church, and organized the Colored Methodist Protestant Church. He died at a good age.

PECK, JOHN, a local elder of Pittsburg, Pa., was born in Winchester, Va., but removed to Carlisle, Pa. There he united with the A. M. E. Church, and for years was the leading colored man of Pittsburg. He was also one of the trustees of Avery College, in Allegheny City, Pa. The Church lost by his death a worthy Christian minister and the community a strong friend.

PERKINS, JOSEPH, of the Illinois Conference, a very

energetic minister, was never known to fail at any point to which he had been sent. He was a man who was desired by almost every charge in the Conference. He died in great peace.

PERU, Ind. The A. M. E. Church has in this town a fine large brick building, which was dedicated in 1874.

·PETERS, SAMPSON, an aged member of the Philadelphia Conference, was a very industrious man. No circuit was too large for him to travel. He went as long as he could go and then asked the Conference to grant him a superannuated relation. On obtaining this he went to Trenton, N. J., spent his days with his daughter, and died in peace.

PETERS, CHARLES H., was born in Winchester, Va. He left there when a young man, and went to Ohio. There he threw his lot in with the A. M. E. Church, and for more than a quarter of a century acted as one of the leading men of that good old Conference. He was compelled though to yield to that disease—old age—which knows no cure. He fell at Lancaster, Ohio, where he now sleeps.

PETERSON, WILSON, a member of the New Jersey Conference, was born at Ridgewood, New York. He was admitted into the New York Conference in 1866, and is now laboring within the bounds of the New Jersey Conference.

PETERSON, DANIEL, a local preacher of the city of Philadelphia, was born in Virginia, but spent the most of his days in his adopted city. He was induced to go to

Africa once, but did not remain long there. He returned home and died.

PETERSON, GEORGE H., a well-to-do layman of Cincinnati, Ohio, has been a trustee and steward of the Church there for many years, and is also one of the trustees of Wilberforce University.

PHILLIPS, WILLIAM ANDREW JACKSON, of the Arkansas Conference, was admitted into the Pittsburg Conference a few years ago; and during his stay there filled some of the prominent stations. He was a delegate to the General Conference of 1880. He was transferred in 1881 to the Arkansas Conference, where he is now filling one of the most important stations.

PHILADELPHIA, Pa. The A. M. E. Church was organized in this city in 1816. There are now eight churches here, Bethel—South Sixth Street, Union—Fairmount Avenue, Wesley—Hurst Street, Zion Mission—South Seventh Street, Allen Chapel—Lombard Street, Mount Pisgah—West Philadelphia, Frankford and Morris Brown Chapel.

PHILADELPHIA Conference is the mother of all the Conferences, and was organized in 1817. It included Eastern Pennsylvania and all the State of Delaware.

PICKETT, DAVID, a presiding elder in the Columbia Conference, was born in South Carolina and was admitted into the Conference in 1868. Since then he has filled many stations of importance in the Conference. He is said to be a well-read man.

PITTEGREW, E. H., is an elder in the Arkansas Conference. The early part of his ministry was in the Ohio Conference. He is laboring very successfully in his new Conference.

PITTSBURG, Pa., is sometimes called the "Smoky City." The General Conference has been twice held here; in 1844 and 1860. There are two A. M. E. Churches in this city, Wylie Street and Allen Chapel. They are well attended.

PHŒNIXVILLE, Pa., is on the Philadelphia and Reading Railroad. The A. M. E. Church has a building donated to them by a company of gentlemen.

PORTER, MORRIS, a local deacon of Lewes, Del., is a man that stands high among the people, and is a great stay to the Church in that part of the State.

PORTER, BENJAMIN E., M. D., is an elder in the Columbia Conference, and at present is stationed at Columbia, S. C.

PORTER, PROF. JAMES, a member of the Mississippi Conference, is a man of extensive information. He was formerly a member of the Georgia Conference. He is the author of a most excellent grammar, such an one as every person ought to have who wishes to comprehend with ease the English language.

PORTSMOUTH, Ohio, is situated on the Ohio River, near the mouth of the Sciota River. The African M. E. Church has existed in this city for some years, has about two hundred members, and valuable church property.

PORTSMOUTH, Va., is a large city opposite the city

of Norfolk. The A. M. E. Church was organized in this city in 1863. The colored people who had belonged to the M. E. Church South, previous to the war, all united with the A. M. E. Church. The church is a fine brick building and the membership is about six hundred.

POTTSVILLE, Pa. The A. M. E. Church has had an existence in this town for more than forty years. They worshiped in a log house for some years, but since then a commodious brick church has been erected, completed and dedicated. Membership about one hundred and twenty.

POWELL, ABRAM, a member of the South Carolina Conference, was born in New Jersey, and was admitted into the South Carolina Conference in 1870. He is now one of the presiding elders.

PRICE, A. A., a presiding elder of the Alabama Conference, was born in Georgia. He is a man who makes a good presiding elder. He moves with speed and is generally at his post.

PROCTTOR, WALTER, late of Philadelphia, was born in Charles county, Md., and raised in Washington, D. C., where he learned the trade of a shoemaker. In 1812 he left Washington and went to Philadelphia to live. Soon after that he was converted and joined Bethel Church in that city. He was married and ordained by Bishop Allen, and for years no man stood higher in the Church and community than Walter Procttor. He attended more funerals and married more people than any minister in the A. M. E. Church. Although not a man of learning, no man was more popular than he, and no one's sermons produced a greater impression than his. Great crowds followed after him when he visited other cities. A few months before he was taken sick, he had a presentiment of his death, and told his family and friends; and when the hour came he was ready. He selected three of his sons in the Gospel to deliver memorial sermons on his death; one in Philadelphia, one in Baltimore, and one in Washington, D. C. His last request was complied with. The morning before he died he called his family together and sang a farewell hymn and asked his wife to lead in prayer; she did so. He then said, "That is enough," and then closed his eyes and fell asleep in Jesus.

PROSSER, GEORGE THOMAS, a member of the Pittsburg Conference, was born in Columbia, Pa., 1842, and was admitted into the Pittsburg Conference in 1877. At present he is stationed at Wheeling, W. Va. No man has done more work than he since he has been in the Conference. Success has attended his labors.

PROVIDENCE, R. I. It is said this place was first settled by Roger Williams. The A. M. E. Church was first organized in this city by Rev. N. C. W. Cannon. For some years the church was a small frame building. In 1865, during the pastorate of Rev. J. H. W. Burley, a new brick church was erected, and it is now one of the finest churches in the New England Conference.

Q

QUINCY, Ill., is a handsome city on the Mississippi River. The A. M. E. Church is one of the largest in the State, and has one of the largest congregations and about three hundred and fifty members.

QUINN, BENJAMIN W., a late member of the Florida Conference; was there in the organization of the Conference; his ministerial career was short. He died in his youth.

R

RADDLE, ANDREW, a local preacher of Trenton, N. J., was born in that State, and lived and died an acceptable local preacher.

RAHWAY, N. J. The A. M. E. Church in this town was organized by some of the pioneers of the Conference. She has come along through deep waters. Several attempts were made to take her out of the connection. She was finally sold and another lot was bought, and a new church built, which is now doing well.

RALEIGH, N. C., is the capital of the State. The A. M. E. Church was organized in this city soon after the late war. Rev. G. W. Brodie was the first pastor. There are two churches in the city now.

RALPH, WILLIAM GOLIATH, a venerable member of the Pittsburg Conference, has been in the itinerant ranks for years, and although quite advanced in life, still keeps in the field.

RANDOLPH, J. W., a member of the Texas Conference, was born in Philadelphia, Pa. He was a teacher of music there for years, and afterwards went South, where he was admitted into the Conference. He has since filled prominent charges.

RANKIN, DOUGLASS, a member of the Tennessee Conference, has been a very successful pastor in every charge he has filled.

READING, Pa. This city is situated on the Schuylkill River. The A. M. E. Church was organized in this city in 1837. The old Church has been removed, and a more substantial one, free from debt, has been built in its place.

REEDER, CHARLES C., a member of the Baltimore Conference, was born in Funkstown, Md., and for many years lived in Hagerstown, Md. In 1875 he was admitted into the Baltimore Conference and is still at work.

REDEX, M. L., a young talented member of the Kentucky Conference, was born in Indiana. After finishing his studies he taught school for some time. In 1875 he was admitted into the Indiana Conference, and then transferred to the Kentucky Conference from which, after spending a few years, he was called from labor to reward.

REVELS, HIRAM H., a brother of Dr. Revels, was born in Fayetteville, N. C., Sept. 1, 1822. He left North Carolina when young, went to Indiana and there received an education. He then entered the ministry of the A. M. E. Church in which he filled prominent charges. He then withdrew and joined the Presbyterian Church, and went to

Baltimore, Md., where he spent some time as pastor of Madison Street Presbyterian Church. Feeling that his health was failing he resigned and went South. There he reunited with the A. M. E. Church. Whilst filling the station at Natchez, he was elected to the United States Senate, and occupied, it is said, the very same seat that Mr. Jefferson Davis once filled. When his term expired he returned home and entered the M. E. Church, where he is working at present.

REVELS, WILLIS R., M.D., was born in North Carolina. At an early age he went to Indiana, and settled in the city of Indianapolis, and was subsequently admitted into the Conference. He then studied medicine with a view of going to Liberia, Africa, but declined to go and remained in the work of the ministry. Dr. Revels was a very popular preacher and filled nearly all of the prominent stations in the Conference. His last appointment was Richmond, Ind. He went from it to Indianapolis and there died, resting upon the rod and staff of the Master.

REX, JAMES T., of the New Jersey Conference, was born in Maryland, but left there and went to New Jersey where he joined the A. M. E. Church. He was afterwards admitted into the Conference and has done good work in it.

RHODES, HENRY JACKSON, late of the Philadelphia Conference, was born in New York State. He remained there until he was grown. Afterwards he joined the A. M. E. Church, and went to Philadelphia. He was admitted into the Conference, transferred to the Baltimore Conference, and then back to the Philadelphia Conference. He was next sent to Albany, N. Y., where his labors were greatly blessed. There he contracted disease and began to give way. Owning a house and lot at Norristown, Pa., he went home and died.

RICE, GEORGE, a venerable local preacher of Philadelphia, was born in Cecil County, Md., but spent the most of his days in his adopted city. He raised a fine family of children. He worked for one firm in Philadelphia for more than thirty years, and when too old to work was still retained and paid the same wages as before. He died at the advanced age of nearly eighty, but still lives in the memories of the people of Philadelphia.

RICE, SPOTTSWOOD, a member of the Missouri Conference, was born a slave in that State and was deprived of an education. Since he has been in the Conference though, he has worked hard and sustained himself very creditably.

RICHARDSON, JACOB D., one of the early ministers of the A. M. E. Church was considered a very able man in his day. He became displeased with some of Bishop Allen's appointments, and left the Church, and united with the Zion Church. It is said, by those who professed to know, that during his last illness he sent for the late Rev. Richard Robinson, who was then pastor of Bethel Church in the City of New York, and asked him (Robinson) to take him into the A. M. E. Church, so that he might die there.

RICHARDSON, LETITIA, the wife of Rev. William

Richardson, survived her husband for many years, and was a faithful member of Ebenezer Church, in Baltimore, and for a long time was the president of the Daughters of Conference. She lived with one family several years, and was much respected. She died in 1867, at a good age.

RICHARDSON, WILLIAM, one of the early ministers of the A. M. E. Church, traveled very extensively on the Eastern Shore of Maryland, and was highly respected by all who knew him. He died before he reached middle age.

RICHFIELD, FRISBY JACOB, a layman of Baltimore, Md., has been a member of Bethel Church for forty years, and served acceptably as trustee and class leader. He is also a great Sunday School worker.

RICHMOND, IND. The A. M. E. Church was first organized by Bishop Quinn, who was the Western missionary. It is one of the most important stations in that Conference. In this city Bishop Quinn lived and died, and in one of the cemeteries he sleeps, awaiting the resurrection.

RICHMOND, VA. The A. M. E. Church was organized in this city soon after the close of the war, and amidst all the changes holds her own.

RIDOUT, DANIEL, a member of the Baltimore Conference, was born in Maryland. In 1856 he was admitted into the Conference, and has continued to travel and labor very acceptably ever since.

ROBERTS, TURNER W., a late member of the Illinois Conference, was born in North Carolina, and went to Indiana and settled. He became a member of the A. M. E.

Church, was admitted into the Conference, and was seen moving across the prairies as an itinerant messenger. He went to Kentucky in 1848, and, although a free man, was arrested and sold at public auction; he was, however, fortunate enough to get some friend to bid him in. The money was raised, and he returned to Indiana to remain until he could go back as a free man. The last charge he filled was Springfield, Illinois. He died there at his post.

ROBERTS, WESLEY, a local preacher of Xenia, Ohio, a man that was much respected, was a local delegate to the General Conference of 1848. He has long since passed away.

ROBINSON, AUGUSTUS, a member of the Philadelphia Conference, was born in Dorchester county, Md., and was admitted into the Baltimore Conference in 1870. He filled several stations in the Baltimore Conference, and was then transferred to the Philadelphia Conference. He is stationed at Philadelphia, Pa.

ROBINSON, JOSEPH H., a member of the Baltimore Conference, was born in Maryland, was admitted into the Baltimore Conference in 1873, and is an active member of the same.

ROBINSON, J. R., a presiding elder in the East Florida Conference, is one of the rising young men of the Conference.

ROBINSON, MOSES, an aged member of the Philadelphia Conference, was born in Delaware. He was a man of no education, but stood very high among the citizens of

Georgetown, Delaware, where he lived for a long time. He died a few years ago.

ROBINSON, RICHARD, a late venerable member of the Philadelphia Conference, was born in Cecil county, Maryland, and moved into Buck's county, Pa., when he was a young man. Bishop Quinn said he found young Robinson at a place called White Marsh, it being a part of the first circuit he ever traveled as an itinerant preacher. One night there was a large congregation out to hear the first A. M. E. Church minister preach, and among the crowd was young Richard Robinson. At the close of the sermon the preacher said: "All you who wish to be saved stand up." The whole congregation rose up. Then said he: "You are all now members of the Church," and further said: "Richard Robinson you are the leader." Next morning the preacher left. When he returned the leader and all his members had been to a country ball. The preacher rebuked them for so doing, and they all started anew. Up to this time none of them were converted, but held their regular class meeting once every week. The leader, young Robinson, doing the best he could in trying to instruct them, found it was hard for the blind to lead the blind, and so they set apart a certain night to pray for conversion. They all met and sought earnestly; that night the leader and nearly all the class were converted.

Richard Robinson was admitted into the Conference and ordained for the work in Hayti. He went, but how long he remained the writer does not know. After returning from Hayti, he entered the field in this country, and soon began to rise. In a few years he became the leader of the Conference. He filled New York, Baltimore, Boston and Philadelphia stations. In 1844 he was a very prominent candidate for the Episcopal office. He said to the writer once—that if he had been anxious for the office he could have been elected in 1844. He further said: "That a bishop ought to be able to defend his Church and doctrine with his pen, and he knew he was not." Frankford, Pa., was his last appointment. He was going out from Philadelphia to Frankford one day, riding on the front of a street car which came in contact with a hay wagon and upset. The car fell upon him, and so mashed him, that he died.

ROBINSON, SCIPIO AFRICANUS HAMILTON, a presiding elder of the Georgia Conference, is one of the strong men of that Conference. He is very popular as a presiding officer. He has represented his Conference in the General Conference several terms.

RODGERS, CAIN, a presiding elder of the Alabama Conference was born in Georgia, and was a slave until the emancipation. He was amongst the first who joined the A. M. E. Church. Since his admission into Conference he has filled the most important stations in the Conference. He has been presiding elder several terms, and is now presiding elder of the Union Spring District, Alabama Conference.

RODGERS, WILLIAM, a member of the New Jersey Conference, was born in Springtown, N. J. In 1865 he was admitted into the Philadelphia Conference, and was transferred to the New York Conference. He is now an active member of the New Jersey Conference.

ROSS, OLIVER PERRY, a member of the West Kentucky Conference, was born in East Tennessee. He was raised on a farm that was owned by his father. Just about the commencement of the late war, the father, mother and all the children left for Ohio, and on reaching there settled on a farm and went to work. They worked in the summer and went to school in the winter. There are four sons, and are all able preachers. Oliver Perry and A. H., are members of the Kentucky Conference, William Preston is a member of the Pittsburg, and the other is a member of the Ohio Conference. They are all able ministers, and great success attends their labors wherever they are appointed.

ROSS, R. H., a young member of the Ohio Conference, was born in Maryland. After he was converted he entered Wilberforce University, passed through a regular course and sustained himself very honorably. He is considered one of the coming young men of the Ohio Conference.

ROSS, WILLIAM H., formerly a member of the New York Conference, but now a member of one of the Texas Conferences, was born in Cecil county, Maryland. He was first admitted into the New York Conference where he spent many years, and then received a transfer to the Conference where he is now laboring.

RUSSELL, WILLIAM H., a superannuated member of

the Baltimore Conference, was born in Maryland. He was licensed to preach in the M. E. Church, where he remained for some years after as an acceptable member. After uniting with the A. M. E. Church, he was recommended from the Hagerstown Station to the Baltimore Conference, and was received, and filled a few charges in Maryland and Pennsylvania. His health then failed him, and he was granted a superannuated relation which he still sustains.

S

SACRAMENTO, CALIFORNIA, is the capital of the State. The A. M. E. Church was organized in this city soon after the State was admitted into the Union, and is one of the finest stations in the Conference.

SAINT CHARLES, MO., is a fine little town, situated on the Missouri river. The A. M. E. Church is strong in this town. The membership is about two hundred.

SAINT JOSEPH, MO., is situated on the Missouri river. The A. M. E. Church was organized in this town in 1864. The congregation grew so fast that they were compelled to buy a lot and build a new church, which was dedicated in 1873. The membership is about three hundred.

SAINT LOUIS, MO., is the largest city in the State. The A. M. E. Church was organized in this city some years before the war, by Bishop Quinn, and has continued to flourish. In August, 1872, the new Saint Paul Chapel was dedicated. It is one of the finest church edifices in the West, belonging to the connection. The General Conference of 1880 was held in this church. Another church has been built and dedicated since, called St. Peter's Chapel. The third church is situated in south St. Louis.

SAILES, SUSAN, was an excellent Christian woman. For many years she was a member of Bethel Church, Baltimore, Md. She died some few years since.

SALEM, N. J., is the capital of Salem County, and is, perhaps, one of the wealthiest counties in the State. The A. M. E. Church was organized in this town about 1820, and has continued to grow ever since. At present a handsome church is nearly finished. The Annual Conference met in this town in 1864, and was well sustained.

SALEM, OHIO, is situated on the Pittsburg, Fort Wayne and Chicago Railroad. The A. M. E. Church is rather small here. The Pittsburg Conference met in this town in 1878.

SANDERSON, JEREMIAH B., a late member of the California Conference, was born and raised in one of the New England States. He received a good English education, and was among the first who went to California, and was with those who organized the A. M. E. Church. He was employed as a school teacher for years. He was also a very efficient secretary of the Conference. His last charge was Oakland, California. One night he had been to attend a meeting at his church and on coming home attempted to get either on or off the cars, which ran through the town. He fell, and the cars passed over him. His groans attracted the attention of some persons passing by, and they took him up, and conveyed him home, where he died in a short time.

SANDUSKY, OHIO, this town is situated on Sandusky Bay. The A. M. E. Church is small here. There are not more then twenty members.

SAN FRANCISCO, CAL., is the largest city in the State. The A. M. E. Church was organized by some local preacher from the East. Thomas M. D. Ward (now Bishop Ward) was the first itinerant minister who went to this city, and properly put the church in working order. The congregation becoming large they bought a church on Power street, where they are now worshipping.

SAULS, SCIPIO, a presiding elder of the North Carolina Conference, has represented his Conference in several General Conferences, and is considered a remarkable man to manage a district.

SAULTERS, MOSES B., a member of the Georgia Conference, but formerly of the South Carolina Conference, was born in Charleston, South Carolina. He was educated at Wilberforce University, Ohio, and has filled some prominent stations in the South Carolina Conference. He is now filling a large appointment in Columbia, Ga.

SAVANNAH, Ga. The first A. M. E. Church in the State was organized in this city, by Rev. James Lynch, in 1865. Rev. C. L. Bradwell was one of the first ministers who united with him. There are two flourishing churches in this city at present, and one mission.

SAWYER, CHARLES, a late member of the Philadelphia Conference, was born a slave in Washington, D. C. He was admitted into the Baltimore Conference in 1851, and died in Philadelphia in 1857.

SAWYER, J. J., a member of the East Florida Conference, was educated for a Presbyterian minister. He subsequently entered the A. M. E. Church, and is now the Principal of the Conference High School.

SAMPSON, C., a member of the North Carolina Conference, was born and raised in Wilmington, N. C. He has filled several prominent stations in that Conference.

SAMPSON, GEORGE, C., a young member of the Pittsburg Conference, was born in Hamilton, Ohio, and was educated at the Allegheny Theological Seminary. He is a young man of promise.

SAMPSON, W. W., a presiding elder in the East Florida Conference, was born in North Carolina; went to Ohio when a young man, and afterward went South. He has done good work.

SCHUREMAN, WILLIAM, D. W., a member of the Virginia Conference, was born in Washington, D. C., 1825. He is the son of the late Rev. Peter D. W. Schureman. He was converted when he was a small boy, and was so gifted in prayer that he was called the little praying boy. In 1848 he was admitted into the Baltimore Conference, and soon began to show signs of future usefulness. He remained in the Baltimore Conference a few years and then went, by transfer, to the Philadelphia Conference, and soon came to the front. He filled nearly all the stations of prominence in the Philadelphia Conference. In 1864 he was transferred to the Baltimore Conference, and built the Ebenezer Church in Baltimore, Md. He then filled Bethel Church in the same city. In 1868 he was transferred to the Virginia Conference where he has been very successful as pastor and presiding elder.

SCOTT, ISRAEL, a member of the New York Conference at the time of his death, was born in New Jersey. He was admitted into the Philadelphia Conference when a young man and continued to labor on circuits and in stations until the buoyancy of youth was gone. He fell at his post, and was buried at Flushing, Long Island.

SCOTT, JOHN B., a local preacher of New Jersey, was born in Maryland, went to New Jersey in his youth, and remained an acceptable local preacher until his death.

SCOTT, JOHN R., late of Florida Conference, was born and raised in that State, and entered the A. M. E. Church soon after its organization. He soon gave evidence of the coming man. He filled a very responsible position in the Government, was a delegate to the General Conference of 1876, and was on the Episcopal Committee. His death was a great loss to the Conference.

SCOTT, WILLIAM, a layman of Philadelphia, Pa., was a member, steward and trustee of Bethel Church for many years. He was a man of considerable wealth. His death was sudden.

SEATON, DANIEL PETER M. D., a presiding elder in

the Baltimore Conference, was born in Reisterstown, Md, 1835, and lived there until he was a youth. He then went to Baltimore, and from there to New York where he joined the A. M. E. Church in Buffalo, New York. In 1864 he was admitted into the New York Conference, where he remained two years, and then was transferred to the Philadelphia Conference; from there, he went to Wilmington, N. C., and then to the Baltimore Conference. He spent three years at Indianapolis. He then visited the Holy Land, and spent some time. Returning, he commenced work in the Baltimore Conference.

SELMA, ALA., is the capital of Dallas county. The A. M. E. Church has about five hundred members here. The mission is in good condition.

SHAFFER, C. T., a member of the Philadelphia Conference at present, was born in Ohio, and educated at the Berea College, Kentucky. He served as a soldier in the army, and went in and came out without receiving any injuries whatever. He spent the first years of his ministry in the Ohio Conference, and then was transferred to New York and served the Fleet Street Church, Brooklyn. At present he is stationed in Philadelphia—Allen Chapel.

SHAFFER, GEORGE H., a member of the Tennessee Conference, was born in Ohio. He served in the army sometime, and was in several very severe battles but came out without a wound. He was educated at the Berea College, Kentucky, and admitted to the Ohio Conference. He spent a few years in it, and was then transferred to the

Tennessee Conference and stationed at St. John's Chapel. He has been attending a course of lectures at the medical department of one of the colleges, and will soon graduate.

SHAW, JOSEPH S., a member of the Kentucky Conference, was born in Washington, D. C., and raised in Ohio. After he was admitted into the Ohio Conference he was transferred to the Kentucky Conference, where he labored a few years. Since then he has been filling out an unexpired term in the Tennessee Conference.

SHIELDS, JACOB, a presiding elder in the West Tennessee Conference, was born a slave in Middle Tennessee. Sometime before the late war he joined the M. E. Church South, but as soon as the A. M. E. Church was organized in the place where he lived, united with her and has been a successful worker ever since.

SHREEVE, JOSEPH, P., a member of the Baltimore Conference, was born in Frederick county, Md. He was converted when young, and joined the A. M. E. Church. He then went to New York, and was admitted into the Conference, and transferred to the New England Conference. No member of that Conference ever did more to build up the work than he. In 1879 he was transferred to the Baltimore Conference, and is now filling a station in Washington, D. C.

SIMPSON, CHARLES, a worthy layman of Philadelphia, was born in Maryland, 1801. He went to Philadelphia when he was a young man and learned the boot and shoemaker's trade at which he made a very respectable living.

He has been a member and leader in the Union Church, on Fairmount Avenue, for nearly fifty years. He has one or two sons, who are an honor to their aged father, filling responsible places in the Church.

SIMPSON, JAMES, a member of the Indiana Conference, was formerly a minister in the British M. E. Church, but united with the A. M. E. Church a few years ago, and is regarded as one of the ablest preachers in that Conference.

SISSON, JAMES FITZ ALLAN, a member of the Indiana Conference, was born November 1833, in Fall River, Massachusetts. He was the first missionary of the A. M. E. Church at Suffolk, Va. He was admitted into the Baltimore Conference in 1866, and has been actively engaged in the missionary work of the Conferences since.

SLINER, JAMES HENRY, a late member of the Baltimore Conference, was born a slave on Kent Island, Maryland. After he was freed he went to Baltimore and worked at his trade as a blacksmith. He joined the A. M. E. Church and was licensed to preach. He was appointed to fill a vacancy on the Chambersburg circuit. In 1868 he was admitted into the Baltimore Conference, and traveled the hardest circuits in the Conference without a murmur. While traveling the T. B. circuit he broke down, and in a few weeks passed away to the better land.

SLUBY, MICHAEL F., a member of the Philadelphia Conference, was born in Philadelphia, Pa. He was raised by a Quaker family in Chester county, Pa. He received a common school education. After his time was up with his

Quaker friends, he returned to Philadelphia and joined Bethel Church, and was licensed to preach. He was employed as a teacher for sometime in Wilmington, Delaware, and from there was appointed to fill a vacancy in Delaware. At the next Philadelphia Conference he was admitted; since then he has filled stations in Washington, D. C., Baltimore, Md., Wilmington, N. C., and is now filling an important station in Philadelphia.

SMITH, ALEXANDER, a young member of the Ohio Conference, was admitted into the Indiana Conference in 1873, where he spent a few years, and was then transferred to the Ohio Conference. He is now spending sometime at Wilberforce University.

SMITH, CHARLES S., a member of the Illinois Conference, was born in Michigan, and educated at Wilberforce University. He went into the M. E. Church, and was stationed at Clark Chapel, Nashville, Tennessee, but resigned from that church, and united with the Pittsburg Conference, and was transferred to the Illinois Conference. He is a fine scholar and a very eloquent preacher.

SMITH, DAVID, the oldest living minister of the A. M. E. Church, was born in Baltimore, Md. He was a slave until twenty-one years of age. After his conversion he joined the M. E. Church. As soon as the A. M. E. Church was organized in Baltimore, he was among the first who joined the Baltimore Conference. He then began to preach the Gospel to the colored people in Maryland, and he has continued to travel east, west, north and south. In his day he was considered one of the ablest preachers in the Church. He is now nearly a hundred, but goes to church regularly every Sunday.

SMITH, F. H., a member of the North Alabama Conference, was born in Mobile, Alabama. He united with the A. M. E. Church soon after it was organized in the State. He has since filled prominent stations in his Conference.

SMITH, HARRIET, the wife of Rev. Stephen Smith, survived her husband a few years, and died August 17th, 1880, at Cape May, New Jersey.

SMITH, HORACE B., a superannuated member of the Indiana Conference, was born, it is said, in Kentucky, and joined the Indiana Conference soon after it was organized. While he had strength of body he went through rain and storm, but he is now taking it very easy at his little home in Charleston, Indiana.

SMITH, JOHN McINTOSH, a member of the Indiana Conference, was born in Richmond, Ind., and was admitted into the Conference when a young man. He has worked his way up to where he is. He was a delegate to the General Conference of 1880.

SMITH, JOSEPH H., a late member of the Philadelphia Conference, was born in Harford county, Md. He went to Philadelphia when he was a young man, and joined the Union Church on Coates street. He soon showed signs of future usefulness. The Church having confidence in his Christian integrity, gave him license to preach. He was subsequently admitted into the Philadelphia Conference, and was regarded as an eloquent preacher, and a very exemplary Christian. He filled important stations in his Conference very acceptably. He was very much afflicted with the rheumatism in his last years and was compelled to superannuate. But he was ready when the messenger came for him and died at Germantown, Pa.

SMITH, STEPHEN, a very wealthy local elder, was born in Columbia, Pa. The gentleman who raised him set him up in the lumber business, and he followed it for many years until he acquired a fortune. He was converted during the time that Rev. David Smith traveled the Columbia circuit, Pa. Soon after he served out his probation he was given license to exhort, and then to preach. Subsequently he was ordained deacon and elder. He was a local delegate to the General Conference for years, and acted teller at the election of all the bishops from 1836 to 1864. In 1840, he moved from Columbia, Pa. to Philadelphia, and bought a house on Lombard street, where he lived and died. He organized a great many churches in the vicinity of Philadelphia. The Zion Mission Church— Seventh and Dickerson streets, was built by him, and a part of the debt given to the members. He also built a home for the old people, and it stands as a grand monument to his memory. He died November 1873.

SMITH, WILLIAM HENRY, a late member of the Baltimore Conference, was born a slave in Calvert county, Maryland. He went to Baltimore to live after he was a man and joined the M. E. Church, but afterward married a lady who was a member of the A. M. E. Church, and concluded to go with her. He accordingly united with Bethel Church, Baltimore, Md., and was licensed to preach. In 1867 he was admitted into the Virginia Conference, and was ordained under the missionary rule, and sent as a missionary into Virginia, where he did a good work. He was then transferred to the Baltimore Conference, and after filling a few charges, died at Chesapeake city, Md., April 11th, 1876.

SPICER, CHARLES A., was a late venerable member of the New York Conference. Nothing much is known of his early history. Forty years ago he was known as "Father Spicer." He was a great man to read. During the session of the Conference he never appeared to take any interest in what was going on, but would be sitting off to himself reading. He died in western New York at a good old age.

SPRIGGS, JOHN HENRY, a member of the Baltimore Conference, was born a slave in Maryland, and was once sold South, but managed to get a gentleman in Baltimore to buy him. He got home again in 1865, and was admitted into the Baltimore Conference. He was transferred to the North Carolina Conference, but is now working in his old Conference.

SPRINGFIELD, ILL. The A. M. É. Church has two churches of about three hundred members here.

SPRINGFIELD, Ohio. The A. M. E. Church, in this city, is one of the finest churches of the connection, and in the State.

SQUIREL, ROBERT, an aged local elder of Baltimore,

was born in Frederick county, Md. For some years he was a local preacher in the M. E. Church, but spent his last days in the A. M. E. Church.

STANFORD, ANTHONY LEWIS, was born in Springtown, New Jersey, and received a common school education. After he grew up to manhood he was engaged as a teacher. In 1858 he was admitted into the Philadelphia Conference, and then transferred to the New England Conference. He remained a few years, and then was transferred back to the Philadelphia Conference. He was appointed by the bishops, editor of the *Christian Recorder.* In 1864 he was transferred to the Georgia Conference. In 1867 he was transferred to the Baltimore Conference. In 1869 he was elected general book steward. In a short time after he left and went to Mississippi, and joined the M. E. Church. He left there, and is now in Africa practicing medicine.

STANFORD, STEPHEN, one of the first A. M. E. Church local preachers in Caroline County, Md., was a man of no education and yet was very useful. He did a great deal to build up the Church, and died in 1828 or 1829.

STANFORD, PERRY, G., a member of the New England Conference had been a traveling preacher for some time, but a year or two ago he located.

STANSBURY, JOHN BROWN, a member of the New York Conference, was born in Philadelphia, Pa., where he received the first rudiments of an English education. He was converted when a boy and received into the A. M. E.

Church. After being admitted to the Conference, he spent some time in Kentucky and then in Ohio. He was a member of the General Conferences of 1876 and 1880. He is considered a great parliamentarian and has done a grand work at the Bridge Street Church, Broooklyn, where he is now stationed.

STERRETT, JAMES R., a late member of the Baltimore Conference, was admitted into the Conference in 1852 and died at Hagerstown 1858.

STERRETT, N. BASCOM, a member of the South Carolina Conference, was born in Baltimore County, Md. He went into the army and went through the war. He was then admitted into the Baltimore Conference but is now in the South Carolina Conference.

STEVENSON, JOHN W., M. D., a member of the Baltimore Conference, was born in Baltimore, Md. He went to Philadelphia when quite young and engaged in the business of an apothecary. In 1862 he was admitted to the Philadelphia Conference. He was appointed to Oxford, Pa. in 1864, and then entered Lincoln University, where he spent some time. He also attended a medical college in Philadelphia, from which he obtained the degree of M. D. He has been very successful as a pastor and church builder. After building and paying for the fine church in Trenton, New Jersey, he was transferred to Washington, D. C. to build a new church there.

STEWARD, BARRY W., a member of the Missouri Conference, was born and raised in the State of Missouri.

After his admission into the Conference he grew up rapidly and was soon considered one of her ablest sons. He is now working very successfully in the Conference.

STEWARD, JOHN W., a member of the Ohio Conference, was born in Philadelphia, Pa., and went to Ohio when a young man. He was admitted into the Ohio Conference in 1860 and has continued in the work ever since.

STEWARD, MACK, a venerable member of the Florida Conference, was among the first that volunteered to go into Florida to preach the Gospel to his brethren. He was appointed the first presiding elder of the Mariana District. There he labored and there he fell at his post, leaving behind him a ministerial record worthy to be copied by others.

STEWARD, REUBEN, a local deacon of Baltimore County, was a great help to the ministers and church. He was a dealer in straw. One day, after taking a load of it to Baltimore, he went on his way home, but was taken sick in his wagon and died before he reached there.

STEWARD, THEOPHILUS GOULD, was born in New Jersey, where he received a good English education. In 1864 he was admitted into the Philadelphia Conference. In 1865 he was transferred to the South Carolina Conference and was present at its organization. He spent a few years in South Carolina and then went to Georgia, where he was pastor as well as presiding elder. He was at one time cashier of the Freedman's bank. On leaving Georgia he went as missionary to Hayti, but remained there only a short time. He returned home and assumed the pastorate, and while filling the Zion mission station in Philadelphia, entered an Episcopal theological college and graduated therefrom with the highest honors. He is now stationed in Wilmington, Delaware.

STEWARD, T. McCANTS, a member of the New Jersey Conference, was born in South Carolina, and after receiving an education was admitted to the bar and for some time practiced law, but feeling it his duty to preach the gospel he left the bar and went into the South Carolina Conference. Wishing to complete a course of theology, he obtained a transfer to the New Jersey Conference. He was stationed at Princeton, New Jersey, and there went through the theological seminary. At present he is stationed at the Sullivan Street Church, New York, and his success has been grand.

STEWARD, WILLIAM G., P. M., of the East Florida Conference, was born in Georgia. He was among the first that entered the A. M. E. Church Conference when organized, and has filled the position of pastor and presiding elder. He has also been the postmaster of the city of Tallahassee, Florida, for eight years, and has given general satisfaction.

STRANGE, JACKLIN, a member of the Baltimore Conference at present, but formerly of the Virginia Conference, was born in Winchester, Virginia, and admitted into the Baltimore Conference in 1867. When the Virginia Conference was organized in Richmond, Virginia, he was among the first that composed it. He was appointed to

Staunton, Virginia, and succeeded in building the first A. M. E. Church in that town. He has filled very important stations in the Virginia Conference as pastor and has been presiding elder. He was also a delegate to the General Conferences of 1872 and 1876. He is now working in the bounds of the Baltimore Conference.

STRAWS, STRADFORD, a member of the Kentucky Conference, was born a slave in Kentucky, and as strange as it may appear, received a good English education, which was given by his master. He was a member of the M. E. Church South before the war. He was among the first to unite with the A. M. E. Church in that part of Kentucky. He has been successful as a pastor wherever he has been appointed.

STRINGER, THOMAS W., M. D., a member of the North Mississippi Conference, was for some years a minister in Canada. After the war he went down the Mississippi Valley, and there has worked for the good of his race and the Church, and has accomplished a great deal in that direction.

STOKES, DARIUS, a local deacon of Baltimore, was born and raised in that city and was one of the ablest debaters the Church ever had. As a business man he had few equals. He took a notion to go to California, where he spent several years. He died in Virginia City, Nevada.

STOKES, LEMUEL, a member of the Indiana Conference, was born in Tennessee, December 19, 1833, and was admitted into the Indiana Conference in 1871. Since then he has been actively engaged in the work, filling acceptably circuits and stations.

STOKES, JOHN W., a very talented local preacher, was born in Baltimore, Maryland. After he grew to be a man he went to Philadelphia and spent several years. He finally concluded to go to Canada, and there he died.

STUBBS, HARRY, a late member of the Alabama Conference, was born in Columbus, Georgia. At an early age he entered the M. E. Church and was there licensed to preach. He was among the first who united with the A. M. E. Church in the city of Columbus, Georgia, and he was admitted into the South Carolina Conference in 1865. When the Georgia Conference was organized in 1867 in Macon, Georgia, he was sent into Alabama and there raised the flag of African Methodism. After laboring in that State for several years he ended his career at Selma, Alabama.

T

TALLEY, ROBERT, a member of the West Tennessee Conference, was born in Tennessee and has been in the Conference for some time.

TANNER, BENJAMIN T., D. D., editor of the *Christian Recorder*, was born in Pittsburg, Pennsylvania, December 25, 1835. He was educated at Avery College, Allegheny City. In 1860 he was appointed missionary to California, but failed to go. He supplied the Fifteenth Street Presbyterian Church, Washington, D. C. In 1863 he was admitted into the Baltimore Conference and was elected secretary of the General Conference of 1868, and then elected editor of the *Christian Recorder*. He has been re-elected at every General Conference since. At the present writing he is in Europe.

TANNER, LETHIA, a remarkable Christian woman, was one of the strong supporters of the Church in Washington, D. C. For years she was regarded as the mother of the Church, and lived to be an old lady and died a member of Union Bethel Church.

TAYLOR, BARTLETT, a member of the Kentucky Conference, was born in Louisville, Kentucky, and for years did a flourishing business as a butcher. He was among the first that responded to the cause of African Methodism in his native city, and since he has been in the Conference is styled the great church builder, for wherever he has been stationed he has done something in that direction.

TENNESSEE CONFERENCE was organized in 1868. It then included all the State of Tennessee. In 1876 the Conference was divided into the Tennessee and West Tennessee Conferences.

TERRE HAUTE, INDIANA. The African M. E. Church has existed in this city for many years. In 1874 a new church was dedicated in this city. Membership about 200.

TEXAS CONFERENCE was organized in 1868. It then embraced the whole State. Since that time it has been divided into three conferences.

THOMAS, C. O. H., A. M., of the West Tennessee Conference, was born in the West Indies. On coming to this country he was employed as a teacher. He then entered the Kentucky Conference, and was subsequently transferred to the Tennessee Conference. He has been the secretary for several years. He was also a delegate to the General Conference of 1880.

THOMAS, JEREMIAH H., late an aged member of the Ohio Conference, was one of the early Western pioneers, and traveled very extensively in Ohio, Indiana and Michigan, and died at a good age.

THOMAS, JEREMIAH R. V., late an aged member of the Louisiana Conference, was born in Cambridge, Maryland, and was raised and educated in Philadelphia. He was admitted into the New Conference. Since then he has filled stations in Baltimore, Washington, Portsmouth, Va., and New Orleans, Louisiana.

THOMAS, JOHN, a layman of Bethel Church, Baltimore, Maryland, at the time of his death was one of the oldest members of the church. He was considered one of the most exemplary Christians of his day. He went down to his grave a ripe stock of corn.

THOMAS, JOHN FRANCIS, a member of the North Carolina Conference was born in Washington, D. C., was admitted into the Baltimore Conference in 1846 and spent a few years in that Conference, and then he went to Hayti. He remained there several years and then returned to the United States and joined the New England Conference.

After spending a few years there he was transferred to the Philadelphia Conference. He is now stationed at Raleigh, North Carolina.

THOMAS, NATHAN C. B., a local elder of New York, was born a slave in Prince George's County, Maryland. He left Maryland for New York, in the morning of his youth, and on reaching there joined the A. M. E. Church. He was licensed to preach and then admitted into the New York Conference and traveled extensively for some years. He then located and settled in Weeksville, New York, where he accumulated considerable property. There he spent his days and died in peace.

THOMAS, WILLIAM H., a member of the New England Conference was born in New York and educated at Lincoln University, Pennsylvania. After he graduated he was ordained and installed pastor of a Presbyterian Church in Pittsburg, Pennsylvania. He resigned from there and returned to New York. In 1878 he was received into the New York Conference and transferred to the New England Conference and appointed to Newport, Rhode Island, where he has accomplished a grand work.

THOMAS, WILLIAM M., a presiding elder of the Columbia Conference, South Carolina, was born in South Carolina and entered the Conference soon after its organization. He has filled many stations of prominence and has also represented his county in the State legislature. He has been a delegate to the General Conference several times.

THOMAS, WILLIAM M. G., was at the time of his

death a member of the New York Conference. He was born in Washington, D. C., but left there when he was a young man and went to Philadelphia and then to New York. In the latter place he was admitted into the Conference and appointed to a mission in the East. He was not there long before his health gave away and he was compelled to give up his charge. He went home and died.

THOMAS, WILLIAM, a very venerable local preacher of Washington, D. C., was the father of William M. G. Thomas, late of the New York Conference, and John F. Thomas, now of the North Carolina Conference. The old warrior was a man of no education but a pattern of piety. He died well.

THOMPSON, EDWARD T., a late member of the New York Conference, was born in New York State and was raised among what was known as the New York Dutch. He learned their language and it was a long time before he could speak English so that he could be understood. He entered the Conference when he was a middle aged man, and his ministerial career was not very long. After a few years in the work he was compelled to retire. In a year or two he went to sleep in death.

THOMPSON, HENRY H., a member of the Indiana Conference, was born in Kentucky. He was admitted into the Indiana Conference in 1874, and has done good work in every charge he has filled.

THOMPSON, JOSEPH S., a member of the Philadelphia Conference, was born in New Jersey. He was educated at Lincoln University, and entered the ministry of the Presbyterian Church. He subsequently resigned and entered the Conference of the A. M. E. Church, and has been very acceptable as a minister in the several charges he has filled. At present he is filling the pulpit of the Mother Church in Philadelphia.

THOMPSON, SOLOMON H., a late member of the Ohio Conference, was born in Brownsville, Pa., and entered the Conference when he was a young man. During his itinerant ministry he filled nearly all the prominent stations in the Ohio Conference. The last station he filled was New Richmond, Ohio; there he preached his last sermon. He said when dying: "This is what I have been living for."

THOMPSON, THEODORE ALEXANDER, of the Ohio Conference, was born in Titusville, Pa. After entering the Pittsburg Conference he had an opportunity of studying at the Theological Seminary in Allegheny City, and he embraced it, completed the course and passed a creditable examination. He filled the Wylie Avenue charge in Pittsburg, and was then transferred to the Ohio Conference and appointed to Columbus, where he paid off the debt in less than nine months.

THOMPSON, THOMAS, a member of the East Florida Conference, was born in Centreville, Md., 1841, and admitted into the East Florida Conference in 1873. He is now stationed at Lake City, Florida. He is a great worker.

THOMPSON, WALTER, the secretary of the New Jersey Conference, was admitted into the Conference a few years ago, but was not considered a very brilliant young man. By his industry though, he has pushed his way on until he now ranks among the leading men of the Conference.

TIBBS, JOHN, a late member of the Ohio Conference, was born in Kentucky, and entered the Conference when he was a young man and soon came into prominence. He had the good fortune to be stationed for two years in Allegheny City, Pa., and while there attended the Theological Seminary and made great proficiency. The Professor represented him as one of the most brilliant students in the class. After leaving the city of Allegheny, Pa., he was appointed to another field of labor in the Conference. He attended the General Conference of 1864 in the city of Philadelphia, and distinguished himself in several debates upon the Conference floor. In 1865 his health failed and he was compelled to give up his charge. For sometime he cherished a hope of recovering, but He who controls the destinies of all men ordered otherwise. In 1866 he closed his career.

TILL, ANDREW, a late member of the Philadelphia Conference, was born in Delaware. In 1848 he was admitted into the Philadelphia Conference, where he labored very successfully for years. In his seventieth year he was compelled to retire from active work. He spent his last days at Seaford, Delaware, where he died in hope of immortality beyond the grave.

TILLMAN, LEVIN, at one time a member of the

New York Conference, was born in Caroline County, Md. He left there when he was a young man and went to Philadelphia. In 1843 he was admitted into the New York Conference where he remained for a few years. He then organized an Independent Methodist Church, but it did not continue long. He died in 1863.

TIMOTHY, B. W., a member of the Baltimore Conference, was born in the Island of Tobago, West Indies, and admitted into the New Jersey Conference 1876.

TINNEY, POMPEY, a local elder of Washington, D. C., joined the M. E. Church when he was a young man, and was ordained a deacon in that Church. In 1851 he joined Union Bethel Church, Washington, D. C., and was ordained an elder in 1854. He died in 1865.

TITUS, RICHARD, a member of the Indiana Conference, was born in New York State. In 1867 he was admitted into the New York Conference. In 1876 he was transferred to the Indiana Conference where he is laboring very successfully.

TODD, SAMUEL, one of the old ministers of the A. M. E. Church, was born in Caroline County, Md. He was a local preacher in the M. E. Church for some years. Rev. Shadrack Bassett, the first A. M. E. minister who visited that part of the State, hearing of him, went to his farm and found him out in the field ploughing. He called to him to turn out his team, he did so. They went to the house and talked over the situation, and then and there Samuel Todd agreed to join the A. M. E. Church. He filled several important charges and died in Philadelphia, 1837.

TODD, THOMAS, was a very extraordinary layman of Philadelphia. He was known as Father Todd, and used to say in lovefeast he believed in rule and order. His last days were his best.

TOLEDO, OHIO is a rapid growing city. The A. M. E. Church has had an existence here for some years. It was organized in 1851. In 1864 a new church was built on Era Street.

TOLIVER, PHILLIP, of the Ohio Conference, was raised and educated in Cincinnati, Ohio. For years before he entered the ministry he was employed in one of the banks of the city. Since he entered the Conference he has filled very important stations, and as a preacher no one is more popular than he. At present he is filling very acceptably the station at Urbana, Ohio. He was a delegate to the General Conference of 1880.

TOWSON, JAMES, one of the early ministers of the A. M. E. Church, was born a slave in Maryland. After he was purchased and admitted into the Conference, he was appointed by Bishop Allen to Philadelphia City, and other important charges. As a preacher he had but few equals in his day. He died in Philadelphia, Pa.

TOWNSEND, JAMES M., the present very efficient Secretary of the Missionary Society of the A. M. E. Church, was born, raised and educated in Oxford, Ohio. He was a soldier in the late war, and when he was discharged came home and was employed as a teacher in the public school in Evansville, Indiana. He was appointed by the Bishop to supply Richmond station, Indiana. In 1873 he was admitted into the Indiana Conference, and soon he began to rise in the estimation of his brethren, who sent him to the General Conference as soon as he was eligible. In 1878 he was appointed by the Bishop the secretary of the Missionary Society. In 1880, at the General Conference, he was elected to the position of secretary of the Missionary Society, and he has done a grand work. He was selected by the bishops as a delegate to the Ecumenical Council at London.

TRENTON, NEW JERSEY, is the capital of the State, and is one of the oldest appointments of the A. M. E. Church. The first church was a small stone building. It was torn down some years ago and a large brick one was erected. Since then a very fine church has been built during the pastoral term of Rev. John W. Stevenson, M. D.

TRIPLETT, ISAAC NEWTON, was born in Iowa. When a call was made for colored soldiers, he was among those who volunteered. He went to the war and had the good fortune to come out unharmed. On his return home he was admitted into the Missouri Conference where he spent a few years. He was then transferred to the California Conference and stationed at San Francisco and Sacramento cities. He has since returned home to his former Conference, into which he has been gladly received.

TUDAS, JONATHAN, a layman of Philadelphia, Pa., was born in Salem, N. J. He went to Philadelphia when he was a young man. It is said he was present at the Convention in 1816 when the A. M. E. Church was organized.

He was also present the Sunday morning when Richard Allen was ordained Bishop. He spent his last days in the A. M. E. Church, situated on Hurst Street, Philadelphia. In many respects, he was a remarkable man.

TURNER, HENRY COOK, a very able minister, was born in the State of Delaware, but left it when a young man and went to New Jersey. There he was received into the A. M. E. Church and licensed to preach. He was appointed to supply a vacancy on the Salem Circuit, New Jersey, as the colleague of Rev. Noah C. W. Cannon. At the next session of the Philadelphia Conference he was admitted, and for years filled very responsible positions. In 1843 he was transferred from the Philadelphia to the Baltimore Conference, where he spent two years. In 1845 he was removed from Baltimore to Washington, D. C., and stationed at Israel Church. He commenced his year's work in April and continued until sometime in the month of August, when one night he was taken with something like a cramp colic which baffled the skill of the doctors, and when it became evident that he must die, he sent word to his brethren who were holding a camp-meeting near Baltimore that he was about to lay down the trumpet and take on the crown.

TURNER, JAMES, a local elder of Lexington, Kentucky, was a man of great prominence in that city, and also one who has acquired considerable property.

TURNER, JAMES M., a member of the Kentucky Conference, was born in Lexington, Ky. He was admitted into the Conference when very young, and has proved himself a man ever since.

TURNER, JOHN, a member of the Kansas Conference, was born in Frederick County, Md. He went out West when he was a youth, and when he grew up to manhood he joined the A. M. E. Church and soon grew into prominence. He filled the most responsible stations in his Conference. He was sent to New Orleans and remained a few years. On coming back to the Missouri Conference, he built the St. Paul Chapel in St. Louis. He is now stationed at Kansas City, Missouri.

TURNER, ROBERT M., now of the Ohio Conference, was born in Philadelphia, and was admitted into the New Jersey Conference. He was a delegate to the General Conference of 1880. Since that time he has been transferred to the Ohio Conference and is stationed at Lebanon, Ohio.

TURNER, WILLIAM H., a late member of the Philadelphia Conference, was born in Hagerstown, Md. After his admission into the Conference he was sent to the State of Delaware and in a few years finished his course.

TURPIN, LUNDON W., a local deacon of New York, was born and raised in South Carolina. He went to New York when a young man and there spent his days.

TURPIN, NELSON HARMAN, was born in Delaware. He went to Philadelphia when a young man and entered the ministry of the Zion Church. In 1854 he was received into the Ohio Conference of the A. M. E. Church, and is at present in the South Carolina Conference.

TYLER, PAGE, a member of the West Tennessee Conference is one of the fathers of the Conference and one of the most successful pastors in the Conference. He is at present one of the pastors of the City of Memphis, Tenn.

TYRE, EVANS, a young minister of the Tennessee Conference, was born a slave in Tennessee. Since his admission into the Conference, he has been industrious, and has spent some time at the Central College. He is a man of excellent mind.

U

UNDERWOOD, JOHNSON P., a member of the Ohio Conference, was born in Mount Pleasant, Ohio, and there received his education. Since his admission into the Ohio Conference he has filled nearly all of the prominent stations, and for many years has performed acceptably the office of secretary of the Conference.

UNDERHILL, SAMUEL, a local deacon of Reading, Pa., was born and raised in Pennsylvania. He has been a great support to the Church in Reading for many years, and is considered by all who know him as a Christian man.

URBANA, Ohio, is a beautiful place, and a junction of two or three railroads. The A. M. E. Church was first built here about 1834, and like many other churches has had its troubles. In 1877 the present church was finished and dedicated.

V

VICKSBURG, Miss., is situated on the Mississippi River. The A. M. E. Church has been organized here since the war and is now one of the strongholds of African Methodism in the State.

VINCENNES, Ind., is situated on the Wabash River, and is said to be one of the oldest towns in the State. The A. M. E. Church was organized here by Bishop Quinn, and a new church was built here a few years ago, and it is now one of the finest charges in the Conference.

VIRGINIA Conference of the A. M. E. Church was organized in the City of Richmond, in May, 1877. It includes all the State east of the Allegheny Mountains.

W

WACO, Texas. The A. M. E. Church has only existed here a few years and is in good condition. A college has been recently established here under the control of the Conference. Bishop R. H. Cain is the President.

WALKER, MOORE, a very able local preacher of Philadelphia, went to Hayti and died.

WARD, CATO, a very useful local deacon of Washington, D. C., was one of the founders and supporters of the St. Paul Chapel, South Washington, D. C.

WARE, DAVID, a local deacon of Philadelphia, Pa., was born and raised in New Jersey, and there received his education. On coming to Philadelphia, he joined the

A. M. E. Church, and for years was the secretary of the Annual Conference. He was also one of the secretaries of the General Conference of 1840 and 1844. He died in Philadelphia in 1849.

WARREN, JOHN A., of the Ohio Conference, was born in Baltimore, Md., joined the A. M. E. Church in Philadelphia and was there licensed. In 1848 he went West and was admitted into the Indiana Conference where he remained several years. He was then transferred to the Ohio Conference. After laboring extensively in that Conference he desired to come to Baltimore, and was accordingly transferred to the Baltimore Conference. He left Cleveland, Ohio, for his new field of labor, and reached Baltimore apparently in his usual health, but that very night was prostrated by sickness and never recovered. The afternoon he died his wife was talking about taking him out to ride. He asked her what time would she be back? She said, "soon." He then said, " you must be back by 5 o'clock." There was the appearance of a rain shower coming up, and therefore they did not go. His wife called him to the back window to look at the clouds that were gathering. He looked out at them, and then he was assisted back to his room. He sat down upon the sofa, when there was a sudden clap of thunder, and in a minute or two he was gone.

WASHINGTON, Pa. The African M. E. Church was organized here in 1818 and they continued to worship in a small house. In 1876 they purchased a large brick church from the trustees of the M. E. Church. Membership about one hundred and twenty-five.

WATERS, GILBERT T., a member of the New Jersey Conference, was born in Somerset County, Md. In 1862 he was admitted into the Baltimore Conference and appointed to a circuit in Delaware. Since then he has filled charges in Pennsylvania and New Jersey.

WATERS, JAS. C., a member of the Florida Conference, was born in Baltimore, Md., and graduated from the Lincoln University in 1870. He was admitted into the Baltimore Conference the same year, and was then transferred to the Kentucky Conference and has spent his time South.

WATERS, WILLIAM HENRY, the oldest traveling minister in the Baltimore Conference was born in Calvert County, Md. His parents died when he was quite young. He was then thrown upon his own resources for a living. He went to Baltimore and found employment, joined the A. M. E. Church and soon began to show signs of future usefulness. In 1842 he was admitted into the Baltimore Conference, and with the exception of one year, which he spent at Newberne, N. C., has been at work in his old Conference. He has filled important stations in the Conference and is still found in the front ranks leading on the host.

WATKINS, RICHARD R., a local elder of Baltimore, Md., was born in Baltimore and educated by his father, the late Rev. William Watkins, who was considered one of the best teachers in Baltimore in those days. He was licensed and ordained in the Second Advent Church. When that church went down he united with the A. M. E. Church and in it died.

WATKINS, GEORGE THOMPSON, D. D., of the Virginia Conference, a son of the late Rev. William Watkins, was born in Baltimore, and like his brother Richard, was educated by his father. He was licensed in 1855, and admitted into the Baltimore Conference in 1864. He has filled all the charges of importance in the Conference. No minister in the Conference can excel him in raising money to pay off church debts. He was appointed to Norfolk, Va., in 1880, and found that church six thousand dollars in debt, but in ten months paid every cent.

WATSON, ALEX., a young member of the Philadelphia Conference, was born and raised in Mercersburg, Pa. After spending a few years in the work, his health broke down and he was compelled to retire from active work.

WATSON, BENJAMIN FRANKLIN, the present Commissioner of Education of the A. M. E. Church, was born a slave in Missouri. When he grew up to be a man he ran away and went into the army, and was regarded as a very brave soldier. After leaving the army he was admitted into the Missouri Conference. As an evangelist, he has great success wherever he goes; being a very sweet singer, he attracts crowds.

WATSON, WILLIAM M., the oldest elder in the New Jersey Conference, was born in Delaware. He was first admitted into the New York Conference. Since then he has worked in the New York, Philadelphia and New Jersey Conferences.

WATTS, ANNA, one of the oldest female members of Bethel Church, Baltimore, Md., lived to a good age. No woman was more respected than she, and when the time came for her to die she was ready.

WATTS, SAMUEL, a member of the Pittsburgh Conference, was born in Baltimore, Md., and was admitted into the Baltimore Conference in 1843, and for years filled stations in Baltimore and Washington, D. C. In 1858 he was transferred to the West, where he did a good work. His health has become so impaired that he is unable to work.

WAUGH, JOHN, an intelligent layman of Providence, R. I., was born in Alexandria, Va. On moving to the city of Providence, some years ago, he united with the A. M. E. Church, and has been a steward and trustee, and is considered one of the strong men of the Church.

WAYMAN CHARLES HENRY, a local preacher of Caroline County, Maryland, was born a slave, March 25, 1812. He embraced religion when he was but a youth. His first owner died in 1837, when he was sold for five years. The gentleman who bought his time was very much afflicted with rheumatism, and was not able to get about, and so Charles had to attend to everything. When his time was up and he was proclaimed a free man, he very reluctantly left the home where he had lived for five years. He then engaged in farming and has had some success in that direction.

WAYMAN, FRANCIS, one of the first laymen of the A. M. E. Church in Denton, Maryland, was born a slave in

Caroline County, Md. After he was free his attention was turned to farming. In this he was very successful. He had a large number of children, mostly boys. Before they were able to do much work he and his wife worked on the farm themselves. As soon though as the boys were large enough they put them to work. He had the good fortune to learn to read, and so taught all his sons to read. He lived to see all of his children grown up. One son a bishop, one an elder, and the other a local preacher. In February 1868, he died, aged 85. His wife, Matilda, survived him two years and two months and she died after an hour's illness.

WAYMAN, HARRIET ANN ELIZABETH, the wife of Bishop Wayman, was born in Baltimore, Md., December 11, 1828. She joined Bethel Church in Baltimore, March 1865.

WAYMAN, ROBERT FRANCIS, a member of the Baltimore Conference, was born in Caroline County, Md., February 1831. He was raised a farmer. In 1856 he was admitted into the Baltimore Conference, and spent a few years in it, and was then transferred to the New York Conference, and spent a few years there. He was next transferred to the Philadelphia Conference, and filled the station at Wilmington, Del., and then Bethel Church, in Philadelphia. At the present time he is stationed at Hagerstown, Maryland.

WEATHERSPOON, GEORGE W., a presiding elder in the Florida Conference, was born in Florida. He received his education since the war, and was admitted into the

Conference a few years ago. He grew up rapidly and was nominated for Congress in his district in 1880, and was fairly elected, but counted out. He will, however, contest the seat.

WEAVER, ELISHA, late General Book Steward of the A. M. E. Church, was born in North Carolina, but removed and settled in Indiana, where he received his schooling. He was admitted into the Indiana Conference when he was a young man, and filled many of the prominent stations. In 1860 the General Conference elected him the General Book Steward, and for eight years he managed the affairs of the Book Concern. After returning to the pastorate he filled Buffalo, New York and Newark, New Jersey, stations. His health failing he returned to his former home, Indiana, and there died amongst his relations.

WEBB, WILLIAM, a very intelligent local elder, grew up in Carlisle, Pennsylvania, where he spent his early years. He then moved to Pittsburgh, Pa., and engaged in the grocery business. He afterward moved to Detroit, Michigan, and there died.

WEBSTER, THOMAS, one of the pioneer ministers of the A. M. E. Church, was cotemporary with Bishop Allen, and performed a grand work in his day. He died feeling that the principles of the Gospel that he had preached to others, afforded him solace in his last moments.

WEAR, GEORGE, a very venerable member of the New York Conference, was born in one of the Southern States. He was, at the time he retired from active work, the oldest member of the New York Conference. Since that time he has been living in Rochester, New York.

WEAR, ISAIAH C., a popular layman of Philadelphia, was born in Baltimore and raised in Philadelphia. He united with the A. M. E. Church in his youth. As a public speaker he has but few equals, and no man in his city is more popular than he.

WELSH, ISAIAH H, a member of the Florida Conference, was born in Lewistown, Pa. When he grew up to manhood he went into the army, and was badly wounded during an engagement, but soon recovered. After being discharged he entered Wilberforce University and graduated from there with honor. He went South and still remains there. In addition to filling the position as pastor he is clerk in the Custom House at Pensacola, Fla.

WELSH, JOHN, an excellent layman of Lewistown, Pa., was born in Annapolis, Md. He settled in Pennsylvania when a young man and there raised an interesting family of children. He was a great support to the Church in the town in which he lived for so many years. He passed away, a few years ago, to his rest in the better land.

WEST CHESTER, Pa., is a beautiful town, situated on the West Chester and Philadelphia Railroad. The A. M. E. Church has existed there for many years. The church building is a fine large brick one, and is in a better condition at present than it has been for years. The Philadelphia Conference for 1882 is appointed to be held there.

WEST TENNESSEE CONFERENCE of the A. M. E.

Church was set off by the General Conference of 1876, and was organized in Clarksville, October 1876. It embraces all the western part of the State and a small part of the State of Kentucky.

WEST, WILLIAM C., a late member of the Pittsburg Conference, was at the time of his death one of the oldest ministers in the Conference. When his health failed he retired to his comfortable home in Monongahela City, and there waited until his change came.

WESTTOWN, Pa., is the place where the Society of Friends have a fine boarding school in which many children have been educated. The A. M. E. Church has had a Society there for many years, perhaps it is the oldest one in Chester County, Pa.

WHITE, FULLER, a member of the Florida Conference, was one of the first ministers that entered the Conference when it was organized, and he has continued to labor very faithfully in all the charges he has filled. He has his home at Marianna, Fla.

WHEELER, BENJAMIN, a member of the Pittsburg Conference, has for some years occupied a large place in the affections of the people and ministers of that Conference. He is considered by all who know him as a modest and an unassuming Christian gentleman. Success attends his labors wherever he is appointed.

WHEELING, W. Va. The A. M. E. Church had a hard time in becoming established here. In 1878, Rev. G. T. Prosser was appointed to the society there, and in a short time laid the corner-stone, and put up the building, and had it dedicated in 1880. The Pittsburg Conference held its session there in the same year.

WHITEFIELD, GEORGE C., late of the Philadelphia Conference, was born in Kentucky and educated at Wilberforce University. He entered the Ohio Conference, and after spending a few years there was transferred to the Philadelphia Conference, and stationed at Bethel Church, where he remained two years. He entered on the third year, but his health failed. The Bishops gave him an assistant, and he continued to preach the doctrines of holiness until his strength gave way entirely. He then with a clear sky crossed the river to the better land.

WILBERFORCE UNIVERSITY is situated three miles from the City of Xenia, Green County, Ohio. It is under the patronage and control of the A. M. E. Church. It was originally under the jurisdiction of the M. E. Church, but in 1863, passed into the hands of the A. M. E. Church for a small amount of money. Bishop D. A. Payne was its first President. As an institution it has accomplished a great deal for our youth. Rev. Benjamin F. Lee, a former student is now the President. At the last commencement, 1881, the number of students was near two hundred. Rev. Thomas H. Jackson is appointed the financial traveling agent.

WILKESBARRE, Pa., is situated on the Susquehanna River. The A. M. E. Church has existed in this city for years. The Pittsburg Conference for 1881 was appointed to be held here.

WILKESHELM, JACOB, a member of the Philadelphia Conference, was born in Pennsylvania, was admitted into the Conference in 1866, and has labored very acceptably in all the charges he has filled. He is at present stationed at Smyrna, Delaware.

WILKINS, BENJAMIN, W., a very well-read local preacher of Philadelphia, Pa., was carried away with the doctrine of the Second Adventists. He died in New York.

WILLIAMS, BRUCE H., a member of the South Carolina Conference, was born and raised in South Carolina. He was admitted into the South Carolina Conference in 1867 and filled the office of presiding elder, and also for several years he very respectably represented his county in the State Senate.

WILLIAMS, EBENEZER THOMAS, a late member of the New Jersey Conference, was born in Baltimore, Md., where he went to school and learned how to read and write. He went to Philadelphia and learned the boot and shoe making trade with Charles Simpson. Whilst there he was converted and joined the Union A. M. E. Church, and was soon after licensed to preach. He then went out West and spent some time. Then he returned home to Baltimore and was admitted into the Baltimore Conference, where he spent the first years of his ministry in the State of Delaware. From there he was transferred to the New England Conference, and filled nearly all the stations in that Conference. He was next transferred to the New Jersey Conference. He died in March 1880, at Snow Hill, New Jersey, and was taken home to Providence, R. I., and buried.

WILLIAMS, GEORGE, a member of the Virginia Conference, was born in Virginia and was reared in the M. E. Church South. He was strongly recommended to the Virginia Conference of the A. M. E. Church by the late Dr. Wm. A. Smith of the M. E. Church South. He is regarded as a very reliable man and does good work wherever he is appointed.

WILKERSON, JOHN MILLER, a member of the Missouri Conference, was born in Illinois. He is the son of an A. M. E. Church minister who gave him his early training. As soon as he was admitted into the Conference he came to the front and has stayed there ever since. He is among the ablest preachers in that Conference and fills any station with dignity.

WILLIAMS, GILBERT P., a presiding elder in the West Tennessee Conference, received a fair education and was a school teacher for some years. He afterward entered the Conference. Since he has been presiding elder he has rendered general satisfaction.

WILLIAMS, RICHARD, one of the oldest ministers of the A. M. E. Church, was born in Maryland. He was also among the first that entered the Baltimore Conference, and traveled extensively in Delaware, Maryland, New York, and Pennsylvania. In 1840, he was stationed in Philadelphia at Bethel Church, and was there when the old church was pulled down, and preached the first sermon in the basement of the new one. He died in Philadelphia in 1844.

WILLIAMS, THOMAS, a very pious local deacon of

Baltimore, was born in Maryland. At an early age he united with the A. M. E. Church and continued an acceptable local minister to the day of his death.

WILLIAMS, JAMES MORRIS, a very able member of the New Jersey Conference, was born in West Chester, New York. After receiving a common school education, he joined the A. M. E. Church and was licensed to preach. He was employed for some time as a teacher in New Brunswick, New Jersey, and was subsequently admitted into the New York Conference. He filled nearly every station in the Conference of importance, and also filled Bethel Church, Philadelphia. He built the new church in West Philadelphia, and then returned to the New York Conference and filled the Sullivan Street Church, New York. From there he was transferred to the New Jersey Conference and stationed in Newark City where he finished his course.

WILLIAMS, WILLIAM F., late of the Virginia Conference, was born a slave in Baltimore County, Md., and sold to New Orleans once, but had the good fortune to get back to Baltimore. He remained a slave until the emancipation of the State, but had been a local preacher for years. In 1867 he was admitted into the Virginia Conference and in it worked faithfully. He died at his post on the Eastern shore of Virginia and was brought to Baltimore and buried.

WILMINGTON, DEL., is the largest city in the State. The A. M. E. Church in this city was very small until 1865. Rev. D. P. Seaton was appointed there, and went to work and bought a church on Walnut Street, and then the connection began to look up. In 1868, the Philadelphia Conference was held there for the first time, and ever since that time Wilmington has ranked with the other places. Rev. C. C. Felts tore down the old building and built a new one which, when completed, will be one of the finest churches in the Conference.

WILMINGTON, N. C., is the largest city in the State. The A. M. E. Church was planted there during the war. The congregation first worshipped in the M. E. Church South, but they were subjected to some annoyances, and therefore concluded to go out and build a house for themselves. They erected a large frame building in which they worshipped for several years. Recently they removed that old frame and built a large brick church. There are two other churches in the city belonging to the A. M. E. Church. Membership twelve hundred.

WILSON, AMOS, a member of the Philadelphia Conference, was born in Portsmouth, Va. His father was a Methodist and his mother was a Baptist. All the children preferred the Church of their father, and thus Amos was early received into the Church. He was among the first who joined the A. M. E. Church when it was organized in Norfolk, Va. In 1865 he was admitted into the Baltimore Conference and then transferred to the Philadelphia Conference. He has performed good work.

WILSON, BENJAMIN, a local preacher of Camden, New Jersey, was born in Maryland. He removed to New Jersey when a young man and settled down in the pines of

New Jersey. He subsequently moved to Camden where he lived and died. No man was more respected than he. He raised a large family of children, all members of the A. M. E. Church.

WILSON, H. H., a member of the Indiana Conference, was born in Missouri and went to Illinois years ago. He was admitted into the Indiana Conference in 1869. He has since continued to advance until he is now considered one of the ablest preachers in the Conference. He was elected a delegate to the General Conference of 1880.

WILSON, J. W., a member of the Kansas Conference, was born in Missouri. Since his admission into the Conference he has filled prominent stations. He was a delegate to the General Conference of 1880.

WILSON, ROBERT, a layman of Philadelphia, was born in Delaware. He was a trustee of Bethel Church, Philadelphia, for years, and died at a good old age.

WINSLOW, DANIEL, a late member of the Indiana Conference, entered the Conference when a young man and spent many years in the West. He preached on a certain Sunday and when he closed he was taken ill and died.

WINDER, WM. HENRY WELLS, a late member of the Philadelphia Conference, was born in Springtown, N. J., and was admitted to the Philadelphia Conference in 1860. He filled several stations of prominence, such as Albany City and Bridge Street, Brooklyn. He died at Norristown, Pa., a young man.

WITTEN, GEORGE M., a member of the New Jersey

Conference, was born and raised in Lewistown, Pa. He was admitted into the Baltimore Conference in 1864, and after filling several charges in that Conference was transferred to the Philadelphia Conference. He is now laboring in the New Jersey Conference. He is a little man but is a big preacher.

WOOD, JOSEPH A., a member of the North Georgia Conference, was born and raised in Georgia. He has accumulated considerable wealth, and no man stands higher in the City of Atlanta than Rev. Joseph A. Wood. He was a delegate to the General Conference of 1880.

WOODFORK, AUSTIN, a member at the time of his death of the Missouri Conference, was born and raised in Kentucky. He entered the Indiana Conference when it was small and continued there until the Missouri Conference was organized. He then entered it and stayed until the Kentucky Conference was formed, when his lot was cast into it. He went with his brethren to its session, but was only there a few days before he was taken sick and suddenly died.

WOODLINE, JOSHUA, a late member of the New Jersey Conference, was born in Pennsylvania and received a common school education. He removed to Burlington, New Jersey, and for several years taught the public school. In 1857 he was admitted into the Philadelphia Conference. He was the secretary of the Conference for years. He also filled stations in Philadelphia and Brooklyn, New York. In 1868 he was elected General Book Steward, but subsequently resigned and was stationed at Trenton, New Jersey, where he died.

WOODSON, LEWIS, a late member of the Ohio Conference, was born in Kentucky and moved to Ohio when a young man, and was educated there. He then moved to Pittsburg and engaged in the barber business. He went to the true Wesleyan Church and remained a few years, and then entered the Ohio Conference in which he labored for years. He was one of the best read men in the Conference. In 1877 he was granted a superannuated relation, and went to Pittsburg to rest and to die.

WOODSON, THOMAS, an able minister, was a member of the Ohio Conference, where he lived, labored and died. He left behind him a family of children, who are all fine scholars and devoted Christians.

X

XENIA, OHIO, is a flourishing City. The A. M. E. Church has existed there for some years, and is among the best stations in the Conference. Membership about three hundred.

Y

YIERSER, JOHN G., at present a member of the South Carolina Conference, was educated at Wilberforce University, and then transferred to the New England Conference, and stationed at Newport R. I., and from there he was stationed at Trenton, N. J., and now fills the station at Marion, South Carolina.

YOECUM, WILLIAM H., a member of the New England Conference, was born in Springfield, Kentucky, May 2, 1842. He was admitted into the Kentucky Conference in 1872. Afterward he entered the Wilberforce University and graduated in June 1879. He was then transferred to the New England Conference and stationed at Providence, R. I., where he did a grand work.

YOUNG, CHARLES H., a young member of the Baltimore Conference, was born and reared in Baltimore. He was admitted into the Baltimore Conference in 1878, and judging from the work already done, is destined to be an able minister of the New Testament.

YOUNG, JEREMIAH, a member of the Philadelphia Conference, was born in Delaware. He went to Philadelphia when a young man and settled at Frankford, Pa. Afterward he was admitted into the Philadelphia Conference and has labored extensively ever since. He spent a few years in the Baltimore Conference, but has now returned to the Philadelphia Conference.

YOUNG, HENRY J., a late member of the New York Conference, was born in Delaware. He was licensed in the M. E. Church and continued there several years. Then he united with the A. M. E. Church and remained in a local capacity for a few years, or until 1848. He was then admitted into the Philadelphia Conference and remained in it for six or seven years. He then went to Canada and spent a few years, and then returned to the United States and went into the Ohio Conference, and thence to the Kentucky Conference. Afterward he spent two years in Philadelphia at Bethel Church. His services were then needed in New York to regulate a few things there. He went and performed the work admirably. He improved the church, but was not able to be out to its reopening. In the autumn of 1874 the hour came for him to wind up his earthly career. He said to his friends as his sight was growing dim: "I am dying, I am dying, Oh! my people, my people!" He had got them engaged in a work and he wanted to live to see it finished. Then he breathed out his last. His remains were taken home to Delaware and there interred in the old family burying ground.

YOUNGSTOWN, Ohio. The A. M. E. Church has had an existence here for some years. It is in the Pittsburg Conference and had a session held there once.

YPSILANTI, Michigan, is a beautiful city. The A. M. E. Church was organized here in 1857, and has gradually increased since. It is a fine station and belongs to the Indiana Conference.

Z

ZANESVILLE, Ohio, is situated on the Muskingum River. The A. M. E. Church here was among the first in the State, and like many others, it had many back sets.

But during the last few years a new church has been built and the congregation and membership have increased until it is considered one of the finest stations in the Ohio Conference.

The Author regrets that more of the ministers did not comply with his request in sending him their names; and also that others sent their names too late.

W.

www.ingramcontent.com/pod-product-compliance
Lightning Source LLC
Chambersburg PA
CBHW020928230426
43666CB00008B/1616